Beach BEATITUDES

Beach BEATITUDES

Forty *Seaside Encounters* with
the God of Rest and Restoration

KAREN DORSEY

Beach Beatitudes
Copyright © 2024 by Karen Dorsey
All rights reserved.

Published in the United States of America by Credo House Publishers,
a division of Credo Communications LLC, Grand Rapids, Michigan
credohousepublishers.com

ISBN: 978-1-62586-293-8

Cover and interior design by Jonathan Lewis / Jonlin Creative
Editing by Donna Huisjen

Unless otherwise indicated, Scripture quotations are taken from the Holy Bible, New International Version®, NIV®. Copyright © 1973, 1978, 1984, 2011 by Biblica, Inc.™ Used by permission of Zondervan. All rights reserved worldwide.

Printed in the United States of America
First Edition

With Gratitude to my Daughters

Sarah and Rebecca

In addition to God, this book is because of your love, support, and belief in me. You were the ones who suggested I do something crazy and take time away with God. One of you saw my insecurity and drove me to Myrtle Beach. One of you visited me while I was there. Then you both supported my belief that I could drive back on my own. You freely gave your encouragement, skills, and expertise during every step of this book, guiding me whenever I got stuck, and cheering me on. I am so proud of who you grew up to be. My heart is full. I love you. Mom.

Contents

Introduction	1
Day 1: Delight	3
Day 2: Dig In	6
Day 3: Hand-Delivered Gift	9
Day 4: Entranced	12
Day 5: Further Out, Deeper In	15
Day 6: Let Them Live	18
Day 7: Dwellings of the Deep	21
Day 8: Get Rid of the Bread	24
Day 9: Resculpted	27
Day 10: Front Row Seat	30
Day 11: Second Chances	33
Day 12: In the Twinkling of an Eye	36
Day 13: Merriment	39
Day 14: Sand Castles	42
Day 15: Who Moved?	45
Day 16: Beware the Spies	48
Day 17: Beauty Revealed	51
Day 18: Debris Field	54
Day 19: Shiny	57
Day 20: You'll Know It When You See It	60
Day 21: Clothed	63
Day 22: Cloudy Judgments	66
Day 23: Rhythms	69

Day 24: The Hollow of His Hand	72
Day 25: We're All Looking for Treasure	75
Day 26: Faithful and True	78
Day 27: Split Focus	81
Day 28: Perspective	84
Day 29: Dangers of the Deep	87
Day 30: Colorful Characters	90
Day 31: Foundations	93
Day 32: Simplicity	96
Day 33: The Shoe	99
Day 34: I Can Only Imagine	102
Day 35: You've Got This—You Trained for It	105
Day 36: Jellyfish Sting	108
Day 37: Cheering Each Other On	111
Day 38: The Ability to Bless	114
Day 39: Parting Gifts	117
Day 40: Come Away with Me	120
Heartfelt Thanks to . . .	123

*He makes me lie down in green pastures, he leads me
beside quiet waters, he refreshes my soul.*

PSALM 23:2–3

Introduction

CONTENTMENT SEEPS INTO our soul as gently lapping waves lull us to sleep in the warm sun. In the distance muffled voices carry across the water, soothing us even more. Lazy summer days at the beach speak a universal language of tranquility. It doesn't matter if the beach lines the shores of a lake, a river, or the ocean—there is something healing about being there. Time seems to slow down, and nothing artificial gives us sensory overload. Nature soothes us.

We also know that storms can ravage a beach, resulting in what looks like destruction. Pondering that thought brings us to a realization. Man-made structures may be destroyed in storms. Weak or damaged trees may be blown down; however, that makes room for strong new growth. The beach itself may get rearranged, but it's not demolished. New beauty shines through in a different way.

Life has moments of contentment that we can associate with the warm sun and the lazy sand. Life also has moments when devastation strikes and our life feels destroyed. Illness or injury may steal our physical abilities. Betrayal, abuse, or loss can leave us emotionally damaged. We may even need spiritual rebuilding from doubt, dryness, or hardness of heart—possibly caused by the above.

God wants us to assimilate his truth so that he can use these difficult circumstances to tear down false mindsets, self-imposed rules

(If I were a perfect woman, I would . . .), and false perceptions of others' expectations that have caused us to lose ourselves in the midst of negativity. God desires to eradicate lies so that he can restore us to the persons he created us to be—to let our true beauty shine forth. He wants to bring about in us new growth.

Do you relate? Through a lifetime of circumstances, have you lost yourself? Have you become a hide-it-on-the-outside, broken-on-the-inside distortion of the real you?

I invite you to walk with me and experience the tangible gifts God used during my time at the beach to say, "I see you." I'll share moments when he invited, "Let's just hang out together. Relax and let go of what you think you ought to do. Your only job here is to enjoy being with me and to listen to nuggets I drop into your heart. Some are for pondering. Some are just for fun. All of them are for blessing to restore the real you."

I believe these messages are for you, also. I pray that God will use them to bring healing and restoration. I pray that you will feel the spray of the waves, smell the salt air, hear the seagulls, and know it's okay to be still and breathe. In and out. Until your body stills. Until you hear the voice of your loving Creator. Until the "I shoulds" go away and allow you to embrace rest without guilt. Until you regain yourself and are whole.

> *"Be still, and know that I am God."*
> PSALM 46:10

Prayer: Father God, help us believe that you use difficulties to bring fresh, new life.

Blessed are those who seek God during the storms, for they shall be restored.

Day 1

*The Lord your God is with you, the Mighty
Warrior who saves. He will take great delight in you; in his love he
will no longer rebuke you, but will rejoice over you with singing.*

ZEPHANIAH 3:17

Delight

SEASHELLS! BETTER THAN the booty from an Easter egg hunt, the colorful scallop shells filled the sand and my hands. Happy as a child, I scrambled from one to another and dropped them into my bucket till it brimmed over. Never had I seen so many shells on one beach at one time. Whole, complete, beautiful shells. I wonder if you have had a similar experience. The Pacific beaches I have visited for most of my life had only a spattering of broken shell pieces and, only for the diligent searcher, an occasional small whole one. Nothing like this Atlantic beach.

Long forgotten exuberance welled up inside me from the sheer pleasure of my treasure hunt. With grateful joy I hugged Jesus within my spirit as I recognized this as a gift from him. For, you see, God's purpose was not to fill up a bucket with shells. His purpose was to restore qualities that life had stolen from my soul, like laughter and childlike joy.

Constant criticism steals our joy, our laughter. We begin to analyze every word that comes from our mouth to perceive what might cause offense. But the protection we put up to shield our heart from hurt also prevents good emotions from entering. We end up captive in a fortress of our own making.

One morning, in my captivity of emotional pain from a broken relationship, I prayed, "God, if you want me to live like this for the rest of my life, I am willing. But I don't want to." God heard the simple cry of my heart for him to break me out of my dank, rusty prison one way or the other. For years I begged him to change the other person involved in my life so that the fortress would no longer be necessary. But never before had I just surrendered and conceded, "Your will be done. In your way."

Less than a week later the foundations of my prison began to quake. A major shift in circumstances happened. A chance comment by a friend during a prayer group led me to do some research, and the research showed me connections between what had appeared to be random, unrelated problems and revealed the root cause of the circumstances I had been living under. Interesting fact: When we know the root, it's easier to find answers to solve the problems.

As with any earthquake, I experienced terror. Any time we begin to uncover solutions to problems we must make choices, and oftentimes those decisions are agonizing and take great courage. We come to recognize whether we truly trust God to lead us.

It has now been three years since the first quaking. My self-protection fortress has completely crumbled. A month at Myrtle Beach, South Carolina, represents my first venture into this new way of life. A life that knows God can open impossible doors and will provide for me so I can safely live in expectant joy.

I love it that childlike joy does not depend on our age but on our level of trust that God has our back and really will provide for us each moment. That he can rebuild anything life has broken in us and diffuse any stress bottled up inside, no matter the source. He can give us the courage to change our own circumstances when necessary and possible.

Has carefree joy been stolen from you, also?

Has your heart been shattered to the core?

Are you brave enough to surrender to God in your situation and watch him open doors to restore you—to listen for his voice and have the courage to follow his direction? This is not easy. It may be terrifying to start with. But as you watch him provide, it will get easier to trust.

The Bible says that God will rejoice *with singing* over you and over me. That thought always fills my heart with awe. We are as much a treasure to him as the shells were to me that day. The enemy may say otherwise, but remember the enemy's description. He is the father of lies. So, we get to choose to believe the One who tells the truth. And this is a choice, even though sometimes it doesn't feel that way.

Our awareness or lack of awareness of the goodness of God determines whether we will dwell in childlike joy. What will it take for you to become aware of his goodness as you begin, or continue, a journey to his restoration? A journey upward toward a mountaintop with the smell of pine and the brisk, high-elevation air? Or skiing down a slope, renewing vigor to your body and brain, or savoring a bubble bath or a slip 'n slide or swimming or finding the time to read a book? As you imagine your special delight, ask him to bring you to that place of joy. The place where you know in your very depths that you are his delight. Just ask. He knows your needs, and he cares.

Whether you get a luxurious month or a few precious moments in your special place, remember that the joy he brings is what restores your soul and creates an updated version of the real you. Because he is in the restoration business.

> *Take delight in the Lord, and he will give*
> *you the desires of your heart.*
> PSALM 37:4

Prayer: Lord, replenish my childlike faith and carefree joy. Open my eyes to see you and to believe that you delight in me. Answer the questions of my heart in tangible ways. Give me hope. Amen.

Blessed are those who delight in things as simple as seashells,
for they will discover the joy of the Lord.

Day 2

My goal is that they may be encouraged . . . (and) know . . . Christ, in whom are hidden all the treasures of wisdom and knowledge. I tell you this so that no one may deceive you by fine sounding arguments.

COLOSSIANS 2:2–4

Dig In

AFTER TWO DAYS of filling buckets of scallop shells, I said, "I know it's too much to hope for a conch-like shell, God, but it would sure be fun to find one."

Something caught my eye in the glistening sand. Bending to pick up what appeared to be a broken piece of shell, I realized that it was stuck. I knelt to dig it out, getting excited as I dug deeper and deeper until I laughed aloud, "God, you are too good to me." My hand cradled a perfect four-inch conch-like shell called a whelk shell. I had found buried treasure. Discovery was a major part of the fun.

The whelk shell wasn't the real gem. The real treasure was the love Jesus poured out to me in giving me something he knew would bring me delight. The gift spoke the message of God's pleasure in loving me. Far beyond merely tolerating me, he delights to pour out on me the deep love that dwells in his heart.

Paul tells us that all the treasures of wisdom and knowledge are hidden in Christ, the mystery of God. Why does Paul say that? "So that no one may deceive you by fine-sounding arguments" (Colossians 2:3). These are deeply significant words. In Jesus we find what we need to deflect the lies of the enemy. Through our own mind, through people around us, or through society, lies have been embedded in us.

For most of my life I lived under the lie that I was so inferior and flawed that others—let alone God—couldn't possibly want to be in relationship with me. Early events set the stage, like my mom revealing to me that she had convinced herself that I was a tumor growing inside her, not a baby, because my dad and she couldn't afford another baby. Or like my sister often yelling, "I hate you," when she got mad . . . and my believing her. Later on, other circumstances solidified this belief.

Have you been crushed down to a place where you have come to believe something similar? Once, while teaching an adult Sunday school class, I asked the participants about their greatest fear. The answers shocked me. Nearly 85 percent of the very confident appearing adults revealed that it was fear of rejection.

Here's how their comments went:

- "I don't initiate conversations with others because I figure they won't want to talk to me."
- "I don't invite others to my house for dinner because I am afraid they will say no."
- "I don't invite others to go to coffee with me because I am afraid they will reject me."

It fits, doesn't it? We want someone to delight in us, to enjoy us. Being rejected is the opposite of our deep desire, our deep need, to be special to someone. The implications are far reaching. If everyone, or nearly everyone, fears rejection, no one makes the first move to initiate a friendship. Since no one reaches out to initiate friendships, the lie in everyone's mind becomes reinforced: "See, no one invites me anywhere. That proves that no one likes me." And we remain lonely and isolated.

Walk with me, and I'll show you another glistening treasure that caught my eye years ago: the blood of Jesus. The fact that he died for me tells the true story. One that says, "Jesus loves me, this I know, for the Bible tells me so." It says, "Zacchaeus, you come down, for I'm going to your house today" (Luke 19:3). Zacchaeus, the hated tax collector, was welcomed by Jesus, who wanted to have a relationship with him despite his nefarious profession.

The fact that Jesus died *for us* tells us that he wants relationship *with us*. He doesn't merely tolerate us or see us as an inconvenience. He's not angry with us. He has taken the first step and invited us to coffee.

As with many children's songs, beyond the simple truth and fun contained in them they invite us to explore truth at a deeper level, to dig for more. At the time I first met Jesus, I understood Bible truths at the level of the children the songs were written for, but God held out the invitation to go deeper and to study his Word, to delve into the profound. And so, I dug. Though I have found many treasures, I have not yet unearthed the whole shell, which is understanding Jesus in his entirety. That will happen in heaven when all truth is revealed.

Meanwhile, I still dig. It's a super fun treasure hunt that never ends. I have an extra shovel. Wanna dig with me?

"For where your treasure is, there your heart will be also."
MATTHEW 6:21

Prayer: Lord, may you heal each place where rejection has wounded or destroyed. Burrow into the innermost part of my being and dig out the lies embedded there. Replace them with truth. Give me a hunger to dig deeply into your Word.

Blessed are they who dig for buried treasure, for they shall find it.

Day 3

Now to him who is able to do immeasurably more than all we ask or think, according to his power that is at work within us,

EPHESIANS 3:20

Hand-Delivered Gift

THE NEXT DAY as I walked in the shallow waves, my thoughts marveled at the whelk shell God had given me. My heart overflowed with thankfulness for the beauty of the area and for the special gifts. It didn't enter my mind to ask for more. He had already given me far more than I had anticipated.

Then, right in front of me, inches from my feet, a wave washed up a perfect snail shell. Large, thick, shiny, with no flaws. I didn't laugh this time. I just stood in complete and utter awe that God, the Creator of the universe, would stoop to give me yet another hand-designed and hand-delivered gift.

I realized that the purpose of this time apart from daily life reached far beyond what I had originally envisioned. At first, I saw it as an opportunity to eat and sleep and spend extra time in my Bible, drawing close to Jesus. I did not anticipate a daily personal gift from the King of kings.

I heard him whisper, "You've been through a lot. Your faith held, but you are depleted. Let me replenish you. Let me show you your importance to me, my child."

Do you need those words of life, also? Do you need to have someone acknowledge that you have given so much of yourself for so long that your inner resources are drained? Has your exhaustion reached the point at which you can barely function, yet you have to function because so many people depend on you at home and at work?

I don't know about you, but despite the fact that the Bible assures me that I am important to him, I need reminders. Otherwise, I easily forget my value to him or to anyone else. Let me remind you right now. He sees. He knows. He cares.

It takes courage to believe God when he shows us our importance, but I believe that you are courageous. You can be transparent enough to say something like, "I trust you to show me, God. It's hard for me to see anything of value in myself, but I choose to believe that you do and that you will show it to me."

It's kind of crazy what he can and will do. One time in a grocery store a little girl wandered up to the salad bar where I was filling a plate. At first I thought she was also getting food but soon realized that she was staring at me. I smiled at her. Then she spoke up and out of the blue commented, "You're beautiful."

Huh? God used that little girl to continue to heal a part of me that, up until a few years earlier, had believed was ugly. Yep. Not just average or non-pretty, but actually ugly.

I thought of that little girl the other day when I was feeling sad and was reminded that Jesus thinks I am important enough that he chose to use a random, impossible-in-my-eyes event to tell me so. I asked him to bless that little girl.

Do you love it when God encourages you with the words of a song or something a friend has said? Me, too. But sometimes I need those miraculous little girls. So, just as you have prayed and asked him to show you that he values you, expect the unexpected and accept it when it comes. Don't say, "Oh, no, little girl. You are wrong. I am not at all pretty." Instead, with a grateful heart allow those words and actions to seep into your soul and water the dry ground, to replenish the empty places.

Do you have trouble believing that he will give you special gifts of love unique to your needs? I know he will because I've seen him do it. The gifts he gives encourage us both now and every time we remember them in the future.

As I sat to write this page, I asked God what lesson, if any, he intended beyond the immense outpouring of love at the beach. I heard

Hand-Delivered Gift

his voice speak to me about the thickness and strength of the snail shell and how it provided protection for the animal that had lived inside. He revealed that, for every hardship I have endured, he has built up around me a layer of love, until those layers combined to create for me a strong home, a shelter to protect me. I realized that he was right. Even though at any time my future may seem uncertain, I am cocooned within my house of love. It's from this home—not from the shaky shelter of circumstances—that I live out my life. This fortress gives me confidence to share these words with you.

What about your house? It's under construction, friend. Large, sturdy, and shiny, with no flaws, built with love by the carpenter with nail holes in his hands, the One who laid down his life for his friends.

> *"Greater love has no one than this: to lay down one's life for one's friends."*
> JOHN 15:13

Prayer: Lord, send me a special gift that speaks healing to a stronghold in my life that you intend to break. Whether it's like the snail shell or the little girl, I will receive it with joy.

Blessed are you when God hand-delivers a gift, for you will know that he sees you.

Day 4

The heavens declare the glory of God; the skies proclaim the work of his hands. Day after day they pour forth speech; night after night they reveal knowledge. They have no speech, they use no words; no sound is heard from them. Yet their voice goes out into all the earth, their words to the end of the world.

PSALM 19:1–4

Entranced

THE BEACH ENTRANCED me. Scattered by the waves, shells of all varieties beckoned. Once again my bucket cheerfully cooperated in the adventure of hunting and gathering, while the birds hopped around pecking at bugs and dead jellyfish. The sound of the waves created a gentle lullaby, accentuated as the seagulls cried out in the sky. The air smelled of salt. A few times my gaze came up to scan the water and the people, but mostly it remained on the beach itself, searching for treasure. Suddenly, it registered in my brain just how far I had ventured from my condo. I had been so captivated by the sweeping panorama of beauty all around me that I hadn't noticed the distance.

The way back brought a different story. I glanced at my surroundings but kept my focus on the nine-story building that held my lunch. The trip felt endless. My legs started to ache, my ankles hurt, my tummy growled, and I wondered if I would make it.

Finally, God pointed out that my negative focus was resulting in the problem that somehow felt impossible to overcome. He pulled my attention back to the beach until I again became enamored. I watched the tide pull the waves in and out, exposing more beach with each pull and tossing out new shells for me to examine. "Nope. Have ten of those. Oh, yes. A fragile baby's ear. I'll take it. Oh, I'm back home already."

Focusing on the faraway condo, my trek had seemed agonizing and slow.

Focusing on beauty, my feet made delightful progress that seemed rapid.

Isn't the same true of our journey in life? When our focus is on the circumstances that have broken us and shattered our heart, the journey seems endless—as if the pain will never end. We wonder how we will ever make it through this day, let alone the next day or week or year. But when we focus on Jesus, the One who died so that we don't have to live in those circumstances forever, we begin to notice blessings hidden along the way. Noticing the blessings takes our mind off the problems, at least temporarily. Then the impossible journey becomes possible.

May I share a secret? Once you begin to focus on God, the One who created you and exists as Father, Son, and Spirit, you can't help but want to focus on him more. To focus, my then-twelve-year-old daughter once declared, means to put all your thoughts on something. As you start to center your thoughts on him, you'll begin to recognize his love, his compassion, his might, his beauty, and his active participation in your life.

Wait? What? Yes, his active participation in your life. You'll see how he walks beside you; and, as the famous poem points out, during the worst of times he carries you. You'll see how he speaks encouragement to you and cheers you on through his whispers in your mind, or through words from books or people.

When you need a miracle, like when your injured foot is hurting, he opens up a parking spot directly in front of the store. Maybe you are running late to pick up your child from school, and he blesses you with light traffic and green lights.

Your awareness of him increases. Your encounters in his presence change you. Unexplainable peace fills you during times of stress.

Pastors and teachers tell us that *shalom* means peace. When they elaborate, however, they explain that it's so much more than that, because many Hebrew words contain more depth of meaning than our English words. *Shalom* means:

Completeness

Soundness—safety, wholeness in body

Welfare—well-being, health, prosperity

Peace—quiet, tranquility, contentment, rapport with humans and with God, peace from war.

When I absorbed all those words, I realized that they describe what it feels like to be in the Lord's presence. I feel a sense of lacking nothing, of completeness and wholeness and sufficiency. This assurance feels so amazing it creates a desire to be in his presence even more often. As the old hymn expresses it, "and the things of earth will grow strangely dim in the light of his glory and grace."

Friend, will you let God pull your attention back to himself? Let the starry sky entrance you with the glory of God. Let your heart swell with gratitude for the beauty around you. The flowers, the smells of the earth, the laughter of a child, all come from him. Believe him when he whispers that he will never forsake you. Become so entranced by the story of his love that you glance around and realize that the day or week or month is over and you are better, and better off, than you were before.

Let your step become lighter as you remember the woman who touched the hem of Jesus's garment and was healed after thirteen years of bleeding (Matthew 9:20–22). Shed a heavy weight as you reread the story of the woman caught in adultery (John 8:1–11). The one Jesus didn't condemn because he had come to bring life. Let him captivate you with that same love.

Set your minds on things above, not on earthly things. For you died, and your life is now hidden with Christ in God.
COLOSSIANS 3:2–3

Prayer: Lord, open my eyes to see your wonders. Keep my eyes on you and not on the tough things my day may bring.

Blessed are they who are enamored with creation, for their journey will be filled with delight.

Day 5

"You will seek me and find me when you seek me with all your heart."
JEREMIAH 29:13

Further Out, Deeper In

TODAY THIS WEBSITE caption jumped out at me: DIVE INTO MORE. THE OCEAN IS MORE THAN JUST A SURFACE VIEW (https://oceaninfo.com/list/mariana-trench-animals/). It confronted me with the thought that, unlike me, many people are not content to just walk on the beach and gaze at the surface of the waves. Something drives them further out and deeper in. Under that water, after all, there's more to see, more to know. And they can't rest till they see it.

Mental images of snorkelers swimming above coral reefs among brightly colored tropical fish popped into my head. You know, the kind you see in ads for exotic locations. Ads that tantalize you with giant conch shells and sea turtles. With colorful tropical fish floating along eating plankton. Sometimes the adventurers even swim with sea lions or seals.

Snorkelers take a first step into the mysteries of the ocean. Although they remain close to the surface, they venture far enough out to glimpse the underwater wonder. They see firsthand the vibrant colors and variety of submarine life. I'm told that snorkeling takes little effort but that the rewards are tremendous.

Unwilling to miss even deeper enchantment, scuba divers immerse themselves in the undersea world. They swim right into the midst of manta rays and sharks. Beyond all that snorkelers can see, scuba divers may also sight psychedelic frogfish, neon slugs, leafy sea dragons, and pygmy seahorses. Those all sound like make-believe names to me, so I checked out *scubadiving.com*, where photos reveal that these creatures are real.

Despite the fact that scuba diving takes more effort and more money, these people have a drive that rewards them with deeper understanding of underwater mysteries. They want to experience them firsthand, not from someone else's photos or description.

The call of the ocean draws some people even further out and deeper in. For several years a marine science institute on the Pacific Coast sent interns into local elementary classrooms to teach science. The intern assigned to the kindergarten class I was teaching had jumped at an opportunity to join a two-week expedition in a deep-sea exploration submarine. His video feed connections allowed us to visit a magical fairyland where creatures looked like something out of a sci-fi movie. We saw fish with built-in flashlights (bioluminescence) that allowed them to see in the penetrating darkness. Some of the animals we saw had no eyes but navigated with other senses. His live video and voice connection taught us about what we were seeing.

This made me realize that I have been a surface-viewing kind of girl for most of my life. Scared and timid by nature, I rejected adventure, content to see only the obvious in every part of life. Playing it safe had always sounded wisest.

Skiing down a slope? Nope. I watched (and saw someone fall and break their leg, which reinforced my desire to play it safe). Jump off the rope swing into the creek? I'd rather cling and slide off onto the other bank. In fact, I once climbed up the high dive at the municipal pool . . . and then, too scared to jump, climbed back down.

No longer. I may remain content to look at the ocean from the surface, or by visiting an aquarium, but pondering the hidden mysteries of the ocean has stirred within me a desire to go deeper with God than I have ever gone before. I want my eyes to be opened to see and know more. It's not enough to read books about other people hearing the voice of God, seeing miraculous answers to prayer, or explaining the Bible in a way that makes sense. I want to experience it myself.

My faith years started with staying on the surface, reading the Bible at face value and praying for my own needs. Then time with a colleague changed me. Each time she began to pray she told God she loved him. I had never before heard someone telling God they loved him. From her I learned deeper connection with him.

I've met people who began their prayer time by asking God what he wanted them to pray. The prayers he gave them provided powerful insight into situations. I have imitated that and am now driven to do it more often.

The Lord brought people into my life who knew how to study and discern deep truths in the Bible. I thought this was great for them, but now I want to look up Hebrew and Greek words myself to unearth hidden nuances that our English words don't convey. I want to see connections between the Old and New Testaments that I've never noticed before.

How about it? Shall we ask the Holy Spirit to teach us together as we snorkel with him in prayer? Shall we allow God to reveal his deep thoughts as we scuba dive in the Bible? Shall we discover the mysteries of a deeper relationship with our Creator in the deep-dive submarine of worship? I'd really like your company in these adventures.

> *"But the Advocate, the Holy Spirit, whom the Father*
> *will send in my name, will teach you all things and*
> *remind you of everything I have said to you."*
> JOHN 14:26

Prayer: God, may I not be content to see only the surface of your Word and my relationship with you. Take me deeper than I ever thought I could go.

Blessed are those who adventure beyond the surface,
for they shall learn the mysteries of God.

Day 6

"I have come that they may have life, and have it to the full."
JOHN 10:10

Let Them Live

"DASHA! DASHA! STAY together."

"I'm here, Ivan. Where's Luka?"

"I lost him. The waves pulled us apart."

"No," Dasha sobbed. "Luka! Lu—!" The wave crashed, pulling Dasha and throwing her to the sand. A weak voice broke through the sound of the receding surf.

"Momma? It's hard to breathe. Help, Momma."

"Hold on, Luka. God wants us to live today. Someone will help us." She clung to that hope even as she clung to each shallow breath, knowing that, without God intervening, they would die. The outgoing tide would not return to help them until it was too late."

"Daaaaaaaaaaaasssssssshhhhhhhhhhaaaaaaaa." Ivan's tiny voice tore through her thoughts. She saw something flying through the air and landing safely in the deeper water. Then she felt something picking her up. Before she could be afraid, she also flew through the air, miraculously landing near Ivan. Plop. And to her astonishment, Luka landed right next to her. They would live.

My imagination sometimes runs wild. I wrote this just-for-fun story of Ivan, Dasha, and Luka to give a different perspective of what *really* happened on the beach that day. Which is: A perfect and beautiful snail shell lay on the beach right in front of me. When I picked it up, my hand encountered something slimy and yukky on the bottom, and I realized the owner of this home was still inside. He needed help. So, I threw him back into the deeper water, along with two other live snails huddled in the same place.

Once all three were safely in the water, I wondered how many times God had said, "Let her live one more day," and had tossed me back into the deep water when I'd hit a place of not being able to breathe emotionally because of life circumstances.

I remember one such time vividly. My vulnerable, desperate plea for help had again been ignored by someone important to me. I lay on the bathroom floor in the middle of the night—the only place I could sob without being heard—and cried out to God, wondering if I would live through the night. The pain of rejection was so great I literally thought I would die.

I cannot explain what happened next. A sense of calm suffused my entire being. I heard no words. No Scripture or pictures came to mind. Just a quiet sense of the presence of God. My tears subsided amidst the realization that God was meeting me in that unlikely place. And I knew I would live. I got up, went to bed, and slept.

Just as those stranded snails still had to maneuver through life in the ocean, I got up the next morning still needing to navigate through my situation in the days that followed. But my middle-of-the-night encounter with God changed everything. I knew that he had heard my deepest cry and would give me the wisdom and guidance I had been seeking from someone else. This was one of the first times I truly understood depending on God rather than on a person.

There's a delicate balance between seeking people for guidance and seeking God. Proverbs 15:22 tells us, "Plans fail for lack of counsel, but with many advisers they succeed." But Proverbs 3:6 calls on us in all our ways to "submit to him, and he will make your paths straight." Though I depend on God, I still seek people, with the understanding that, whether it's through their words and actions or about a sense of his presence on a bathroom floor, it's ultimately Jesus who provides what I need.

In the years that followed, new situations arose. You know what I mean. Life is like that—always some new challenge to work through. The difference now was that I knew from experience that Jesus is the

One who gives me life rather than death: physical, emotional, relational, and spiritual life. Now I turn to him first.

How about you? When life upends you and you wonder how you will survive the situation at hand, do you know-that-you-know-that-you-know that Jesus joins you on that bathroom floor and infuses his strength into you? He wants to pour his peace into you because of his unimaginable love.

He whispers verses that strengthen us. He never leaves us or forsakes us but rather walks with us through every life event, providing just what we need. As he matures us over the years, the calm comes more and more quickly. Turning to him comes more naturally. Trust comes more easily. He picks us up and tosses us back into the life-giving water of his presence, just as I tossed our snail friends, Ivan, Dasha and Luka, back into the sea.

> *God has said, "Never will I leave you; never will I forsake you."*
> HEBREWS 13:5

Prayer: Lord, infuse your peace and your strength deep within my innermost being. May I depend upon you.

Blessed are those who give others a second chance to live, for they, too, shall receive life.

Day 7

"My Father's house has many rooms; if that were not so, would I have told you that I am going there to prepare a place for you? And if I go and prepare a place for you, I will come back and take you to be with me that you also may be where I am."

JOHN 14:2–3

Dwellings of the Deep

DOES FEAR OF the future ever rise up in you? Perhaps regarding where you will live or how you will pay for it?

Yep. Me too. Not often in life, but definitely today. When I return after this vacation, my living situation will transition. At this moment I have no idea where I will be. I just know that God keeps telling me to trust him. When fear began to arise today, my gaze landed on all the shells laid out on the balcony. Shells that I have spent the last three weeks collecting.

My grandson's words came to mind: "I feel sad for the animals that lived in the shells. They died." In one of those I-know-this-but-the-truth-of-it-hit-me-hard moments, I realized that every one of those shells I admire for their beauty was once a home. A perfect home designed specifically for one particular unique creature.

My fear dissipated in the wonder of that thought. God provides perfectly fitted homes for every sea creature in the same way the Bible says Christ has gone to prepare a place for me. If that is true, worry is silly. He provides not only daily necessities but also safe and incredible places to abide. Unleashed creativity and artistry abound in the creature castles I am looking at, so I can be confident of the same for me.

Do you like the minimalist look? Remember Dasha and her family, the snails I threw back into the water? They live in what I call "normal" snail shells. A simple spiral with a smooth exterior. In fact, the shell that washed up in front of my feet as a "hand-delivered gift" was a moon snail shell like theirs.

Maybe you prefer more dainty and intricate spaces. Perhaps smaller and more cozy. Augers live in delicate shells with a narrow spiral and a spear-like tip. They range from half the size of my pinkie finger to as small as my pinkie nail. Tucked into debris fields of broken shells and "baby ears," they're easy to miss. I don't understand how a snail could be small enough to fit inside, but God perfectly fitted its home the same way he will suit our homes to us.

Do you prefer a grand space? Remember my excitement at finding the shell of a whelk, another kind of snail-like creature? God's creativity, as demonstrated in both color and structure, fascinates me. Crowned with bony ridges, the shell gracefully spirals inward with an inviting side entrance. It's a mystery how the snail fits around the internal spiral shape, but it does.

Whatever space you currently live in, large and grand, small and cozy, or sparse and bare, ponder this. David lived in a variety of places as God molded and formed his character. Before residing in a palace, he roamed the wilderness, living in caves or even open spaces. Mary, the mother of Jesus, lived in a humble village. Yet both of them found favor with God because of the state of their hearts. God cared more about their trust than about where they lived physically, because that trust meant that their hearts dwelt with him.

What kind of place is your heart? Is it open and inviting to him? Do you trust him for shelter for both your heart and your body?

Years ago our home sat on a hill overlooking a bay on the Oregon coast. One winter an extended storm pelted the area with nonstop rain. Our house literally began to pull apart as the saturated ground beneath it slowly slid toward the water. Walls pulled away from the floor. Earthquake-like damage rifled the driveway and the hillside. We lost our home, and our insurance didn't cover damage from earth movement. So, with no financial help, we needed to continue to pay for the lost home *and* for a new place to live.

God's peace filled me so thoroughly in that journey that when a colleague asked me one day how our house was, I didn't at first know why she was asking. The peace lasted throughout the whole six-week process of admitting loss and the two days of looking for a new place. Yes, in two days God opened up a temporary rental that was empty and ready.

On moving day twenty-eight people showed up and packed and moved us within five hours. That included setting up our beds and unpacking our kitchen items in the new house.

We qualified for a disaster loan that paid off the old loan and provided money for the new home. I still ask incredulously, "How did you do that, God. How did we afford the payments with the old loan and the new one combined?" He gave us a home more beautiful than the one we had lost, and it became my favorite ever home.

More puzzling still: How did he fill my heart with such peace? The Bible calls that tranquility peace that passes understanding.

Sadly, after that time I fussed and worried about lesser things. Till now. Seeing the sea creatures' homes, absorbing God's love at this beach, and the reminder of past provision brought back the deep peace. Go away, fear.

> *Do not fear, for I am with you; do not be dismayed, for I am your God.".*
> ISAIAH 41:10

Prayer: Lord God, may my eyes of trust lift to the heavens, from which I see your face and your hand of provision.

Blessed are those who stand in awe of the sea creatures' homes, for they shall trust him to provide a place for them.

Day 8

Because your love is better than life, my lips will glorify you. I will praise you as long as I live, and in your name I will lift up my hands.

PSALM 63:3-4

Get Rid of the Bread

THE BREAD MOCKED me. For three days I eagerly toasted it to eat with soup or apples and almond butter or any number of foods. It tasted so good; yet every time I ate it I felt sick afterward. Conflict brewed inside me about whether to throw the rest away.

My taste buds said, "Karen. It only makes you feel bad for a little while. Keep it. Enjoy it."

My logic countered, "Karen, this is ridiculous. If it makes you sick every time you eat it, this is not going to change. Saving it makes no sense. Just throw it away."

As I looked up from my kitchen counter, the ocean view captured my attention. Through the open balcony door I could hear the rhythmic waves and the seagulls mewing, and I could smell the salt air. Shells lining the balcony reminded me of the abundance of gifts God had poured out each day. His evident glory and love overwhelmed me, and I began to praise him—for his love and for each gift.

Suddenly, the decision became evident. I opened the garbage can and tossed the bread. Relief replaced inner conflict, and joy arose. The desire for the bread paled in comparison to the goodness of God reflected all around me.

Worship is like that. It puts life into perspective. I can be comforted in sorrow and gain courage to replace fear. I can see what's important over what's a distraction. I can see what is good for me versus what is unhealthy. I sense strength rising up to face hard choices.

The psalms allow us to glimpse David's worship. Words of doubt, fear, and anger transition to words of love, trust, and remembrance. Killing Goliath with a slingshot, fighting enemy armies, and leading God's people all present evidence of the strength he gained from his open and vulnerable worship.

In 1 Samuel 25 we read a less familiar story about the time Nabal insulted David and refused to share the sheep-shearing feast with David and his men in thanks for their protection. In anger David gathered his men and headed out to wipe out Nabal and his household.

When Abigail, Nabal's wife, heard what had happened, she quickly ordered food to be gathered and personally accompanied the servants who delivered it. She bowed before David, imploring, "Please forgive your servant's presumption. The LORD your God will certainly make a lasting dynasty for my lord, because you fight the LORD's battles, and no wrongdoing be found in you as long as you live" (verse 28). She prophesied of God's protection over David and offered assurances that God would keep all his promises to him.

David's response? He worshiped. "Praise be to the LORD, the God of Israel, who has sent you today to meet me. May you be blessed for your good judgment and for keeping me from bloodshed this day and from avenging myself with my own hands" (verse 32).

Abigail's words focused David's eyes on God, and he recognized the gift God had just delivered—the gift of staying David's hand from killing someone in vengeance. David's worship made the decision to do the right thing easy.

Mary received the life-changing words the angel Gabriel spoke. Even though in the short term she might have been seen as shameful in the eyes of her village, she focused on the good. After questioning the logistics of how this unimaginable thing could happen, Mary worshiped. "My soul glorifies the Lord and my spirit rejoices in God my Savior, for he has been mindful of the humble state of his servant. From now on all generations will call me blessed, for the Mighty One has done great things for me—holy is his name. His mercy extends to those who fear him, from generation to generation" (Luke 1:46–50). Her focus was on the promise, not on the obstacles she would face.

The rich young ruler did just the opposite. When Jesus asked him to sell all that he had, give to the poor, and follow him, Jesus understood the hold money had over the young man, who walked away sad. We see no evidence that he ever worshiped Jesus or demonstrated the strength to say no to money (Mark 10:17–22).

Each time I face a situation large or small I have a choice to make—to worship or to remain stuck. Like when my mind replays an unpleasant memory to the point of calling up bitterness, and I am not ready to let it go. I convince myself that my attitude is not so bad and tell myself, *I'll deal with it later*, until the inner conflict says otherwise. Not otherwise about dealing with it later but otherwise about maintaining the hurtful attitude. The Holy Spirit challenges me to praise God for the way he used the situation to draw me closer to him. He reminds me of the goodness of God even in the midst of the painful situation/memories, and, somehow, I am finally able to let the bitterness go.

Just as worship allowed me the strength to toss the bread, it brings me to a place of forgiveness and surrender that places God at the very center of my struggle—the place where he can work miracles. He can do that for any struggle, mine or yours. Let's join David and Mary and magnify the Lord.

> *Come, let us bow down in worship, let us*
> *kneel before the L*ORD *our Maker.*
> PSALM 95:6

Prayer: Lord God, thank you that choosing praise can keep me from things that will bring me, and perhaps others, harm.

Blessed is he who worships God, for his eyes shall be opened.

Day 9

We know that in all things God works for the good of those who love him, who have been called according to his purpose.

ROMANS 8:28

Resculpted

BATTERING WIND AND rain lashed against the balcony slider, lulling me to sleep. Storm sounds reminded me of forty years of winter nights on the Oregon coast, which to me felt familiar and comforting.

The view the next morning, however, felt neither familiar nor comforting. Overnight, the beach had transformed into an unrecognizable, alien landscape. The once smooth, flat beach now featured undulating terrain with winding channels that ended in deep tidepools.

"How dare that storm take away my serene beach?" I fumed. But then the realization hit. Treasure! Storms uncover treasure. I raced to throw on clothes and get to the beach. Sure enough, the channels and hollows had trapped bounty for seekers and protected sea creatures until the tide came in to rescue them. An element of mystery hovered because I couldn't see what lay beyond the mini sand dunes until I reached them.

In the following days I realized that subtle changes to the beach had been happening all along. They were just so minor as to not be noticeable. The storm merely took the shift to a heightened level.

Every day of our lives we encounter events that change us in some measurable way. Most days the changes are minute, but sometimes a storm-level event heightens both the speed and the level of resculpting. The change is dramatic, and often traumatic.

Just as the beach didn't remodel itself, sometimes an accident or someone else's choices bulldoze us down without our permission. Storms thrust themselves onto the beach, and onto us, whether or not we like it, and we feel stuck. We feel helpless. We feel as if the world will never be right again.

We may be angry about the changes—and many times we might say rightly so. The trauma may be so great that we don't even want to look for buried treasure. We may grieve the unwanted changes, but nope, no way, no how will we call anything about the altered landscape good. "You can't make me. So there."

You are right. Our willpower can't even begin to accomplish this, but only the inner working of the Holy Spirit. In *The Abba Formation* Kerry Wood points out that we have been designed to run on spiritual power, not willpower. This doesn't happen at the head level; instead, the Holy Spirit comes to transform us at the heart level.

Beaches swarm with life from tiny organisms, both visible and invisible to our human eyes. Mini crabs and insects live alongside microbes strong enough to break down industrial sewage and alongside good bacteria also found in the human gut. The microbes' job is to clean up the garbage that could destroy life and promote the healthy nutrition that sustains life. The Holy Spirit does just that within us.

As Paul says in Philippians 2:13, "It is God who works in you to *will* and to act in order to fulfill his good purpose" (emphasis mine). I love this. Even when we don't want to follow the Spirit's prompting, even when our will says no way, God can change our will.

Have you prayed something like this before? "God, I know I need to forgive this person, but right now I don't even want to. Change my will, my heart and mind. Give me the desire to not only forgive but to ask you to bless them. Help me cooperate with you." A friend modeled this for me once. When I saw the miracle that ensued, it made me willing to pray similarly for a situation of my own.

You know those things you've desired and prayed for—faith and patience, stronger prayer life, emotional maturity, and the ability to love well? Those are the very kinds of treasures storms can bring.

Once an historic coastal storm blew down three large, beautiful trees in my backyard. I didn't like it at first, but the extra sunshine invited beautiful new plant growth. An emotional betrayal from my sister led to freedom from the control she'd always had over me. Other storms revealed my foundations in Christ to be stronger than I had realized. Recent trials, too fresh to recount, have given me the ability to live one day at a time, recognizing that he will provide all that I need materially, spiritually, mentally, physically, and relationally.

I think of Paul being resculpted when he met Jesus on the road to Damascus (Acts 9:1–19). Zealous for his Jewish faith, he persecuted believers of the Way to the point of death, believing that they were perverting the Old Testament law he loved. Then a light so bright it left him blind, accompanied by the audible voice of Jesus, turned him around. The encounter with Jesus showed him the truth he had been too blind to see. Transformation took place. The zeal remained, but now his passion focused on leading people to Jesus, the life giver. May we also be resculpted by the Master Creator.

> *"Your name will no longer be Jacob, but Israel."*
> GENESIS 32: 28

Prayer: God, work in me to will, and to work, according to your good pleasure.

Blessed are they who embrace resculpting, for they shall be transformed by the Living God.

Day 10

"My sheep listen to my voice; I know them, and they follow me."
JOHN 10:27

Front Row Seat

SALT AIR FILLED my nostrils, and the ubiquitous seagulls again mewed while I followed my mid-morning routine of walking in the shallow surf looking for treasures. Only occasionally did I lift my eyes to the waves themselves.

"Sit down and look out at the waves." The Lord spoke this in a clear voice to my mind.

"Okay, Lord. That's a fun idea. How relaxing to just look out at the water, listen to the roar of the surf, and ponder life."

But I continued to take a few more steps, thinking that I'd do so in a minute.

An urgent sense of "Sit now!" permeated my mind.

Surprised, I said, "Okay," headed to the dry sand, and plunked myself down.

The ocean spread out before me like a giant stage, where birds flew in the air and swooped down to skim the tops of the waves as they rhythmically rolled in and out. I settled in, in anticipation of what God might speak to my heart. Never did I imagine the delight he had planned.

Suddenly, as close as possible to the shore without grounding, something dark soared skyward, tracing an elegant curve through the air before splashing back into the water. A minute later it vaulted into the air once more.

"A dolphin? You gave me a *dolphin*?"

I kept my gaze fixed as it continued to surface, leap, and dive back under the surf before it swam so far away that I could no longer make it out. Stunned, I remained seated for a long time, absorbing what had just happened. The exact timing of God's impression on my heart, and of the dolphin leaping, left no room for argument that God had orchestrated yet another tangible gift to show his tender mercy to a healing heart.

I don't know which created more awe within me, the dolphin show itself or the fact that God cared enough to *insist* that I sit when it became obvious I wasn't yet listening to him. For if I hadn't sat down right when I did, I would have missed the fast and quiet jump.

Did you like that—the way I skirted around the issue instead of admitting up front that I didn't obey God right away? In this day and age, for many people the word *obey* conjures up pictures of a tyrannical or abusive adult demanding compliance to every command they give, regardless of whether obedience would be healthy for the person under their authority. The use of the word itself conjures up the thought of severe consequences for those who don't submit.

But that's not what God is like. Every time God calls in the Bible for obedience, he does so for the good of the people. The merciful, compassionate nature of God revealed in the Bible shouts that we can trust him. We can willingly obey because it's evident that he wants only the best for us. He cares for us.

Do you ever need to be reminded about how much God cares for you? I do. As I sat to write today, my emotions were struggling with a traumatic incident that happened a couple of weeks ago. My distracted mindset left me vulnerable to the enemy's whisper that I can't do anything right and that, surely, no one wants to be around me or to read what I might have to say. Then the wonder of the dolphin moment flooded over me, cocooning me in the warmth of his love and allowing me to see past that lie.

Do you ever want something tangible to confirm God's presence in your life? Something beyond the experience of God highlighting verses to personally speak to you during your Bible reading. Beyond his still, prodding internal voice, do you sometimes long for something you can see or hear? That's why I love the story of God's covenant with Noah and the rainbow sign of his promise to never again flood the earth. God's rainbow pledge is something I can still see today, thousands of years later. And I marvel. That's why, for me, a personal dolphin show freely dropped onto the beach is better than thousands of dollars' worth of diamonds.

I am praying for you right now. Praising him that he knows what speaks to you more than a diamond ring. I'm believing that he wants to give it to you. Because the bottom line is that he knows exactly what you need to fill your heart with life. I am asking him to show you in multiple ways that he loves you and is not disappointed in you. That you aren't to blame for every problem that crops up in the lives of those around you.

I am praying that you will recognize his gifts when they come, whether you feel strong and full right now or weary and heavy laden.

I'm praying that, if he says "Sit down," you'll listen right away and sit with attention.

When tough times come at us again, as they will, let's remember those gifts.

And God said, "This is the sign of the covenant I am making between me and you and every living creature with you, a covenant for all generations to come. I have set my rainbow in the clouds, and it will be the sign of the covenant between me and the earth. Whenever I bring clouds over the earth and the rainbow appears in the clouds, I will remember my covenant between me and you and all living creatures of every kind. Never again will the waters become a flood to destroy all life. Whenever the rainbow appears in the clouds, I will see it and remember the everlasting covenant between God and all living creatures of every kind on the earth."
GENESIS 9:12–16

Prayer: Lord, open my ears that I may hear your voice, open my heart that I may obey you quickly, and open my eyes to see your glory so that I may praise you.

Blessed are those who obey God, for they shall see him at work in their lives.

Day 11

If anyone is in Christ, the new creation has come. The old has gone, the new is here.

2 CORINTHIANS 5:17

Second Chances

MY MORNINGS EVENTUALLY settled into a routine. First thing each day I walked to the balcony and checked the beach to take in the tide. If it was high, I ate breakfast and had my quiet time first, before embarking on my walk. If it was already low, I threw on clothes and headed out immediately. Every day I walked in the shallow surf at least part of the time, enjoying the water pulsing in and out around my feet and watching for shells that tumbled in on the waves.

One morning a beautiful snail shell washed up in front of me. I hesitated because I already had one, and by the time I decided I wanted it the receding water had snatched it back. Disappointed, I watched it disappear into swirling sand and water.

In a split-second conversation with God, I expressed how sorry I was that I so often hesitated to grasp the opportunities he provided. I asked him to help me overcome my hesitancy.

In a miracle that shouldn't have surprised me by that point, the next wave deposited the same shell right back in front of me. Laughing, I grabbed it and danced a jig. I had never before seen a shell return to the same spot once it fell back into the waves. It was as if God shouted that he is the God of second chances.

I can think of many people in the Bible who experienced another chance, people like Samson, Jonah, David, and Peter. But the one that touches me most deeply is the woman caught in adultery (John 8:1–11). Humiliation, shame, fear. A gamut of emotions no doubt raced through her mind as her captors dragged her to Jesus, her sin displayed before the crowd that sat listening to him teach. Teachers of the law and Pharisees challenged Jesus to give her the death penalty.

Uncontrollable shaking deep within her body betrayed her terror in knowing that at any minute stones could strike her body, tearing flesh and crushing internal organs. No relief would come from the agonizing pain until she breathed her last.

The crowd surrounded her with faces that expressed disdain, disgust, indignation, and anger. Unlike an arrow from afar, stoning did not allow for an impersonal death. Each accuser must be close enough to hit their target after hefting and then hurling large rocks. She would die knowing that a multitude of people hated her enough to kill her.

The leaders used her as a pawn to get to Jesus. To them she was a dispensable throwaway. Trash. But not to Jesus. He calmly dispersed the crowd with the words, "Let anyone who is without sin be the first to throw a stone at her" (John 8:7), thus saving her life.

"Neither do I condemn you. . . . Go now and leave your life of sin" (verse 11).

She stumbled away, stunned at what had just happened. The love, the wisdom that filled the eyes of Jesus. The care in his voice when he spoke. How could she not believe in him after that?

A second chance at life. Isn't that what we all want? In the case of the woman caught in adultery, it was her own sin (and that of the man who had been involved) that brought about her need for a second chance. Maybe our past involves a drug addiction or an affair or our betrayal of someone we love. Maybe it involves neglecting our child. Maybe we criticized our husband or children to the point that we drove them away from us.

For some of us it's not about anything we did wrong. It's what was stolen from us, perhaps at a young age: our innocence taken by someone else's choice to molest us, our husband's choice to have an affair and leave us, or an accident that left us with a permanent injury.

Any of these situations, and others like them, can leave us feeling as if life has passed us by or left us with a gaping hole inside. As if we lack the resources or reserves to overcome the grief or depression that came because of it. We can never stop blaming ourselves or those responsible.

In the footnote to John 8:3–11, the *NIV Life Application Study Bible* tells us that Jesus knows our sins (or the sins done to us) and yet offers compassion and mercy. The note invites us to allow his mercy to give us the courage to face our guilt or pain, to allow his love to overcome our shame. Instead of denying that shame or despairing, we are called to be sorry for our sins, to seek the Lord, and to receive (or pass along) his forgiveness.

David had the courage to forgive himself after the baby he had fathered with Bathsheba died. He had fasted while the baby still lived, but once the child died he got up, washed, and went to worship God. He knew that God forgave him, and he chose to forgive himself (2 Samuel 12:14–25).

That's a nearly impossible step for many of us. We beat ourselves up repeatedly. Yet, if we have genuinely repented, God assures us that he forgives. Who are we to withhold from ourselves—or others—the forgiveness he has freely given? (I'll talk about that second scenario, forgiving someone who has harmed us, in Day 17.)

My snail shell now sits on display in my home, where it reminds me daily of God's ability to redeem mistakes—our own or others'—and to give us new beginnings.

"Neither do I condemn you. . . . Go now and leave your life of sin."
JOHN 8:11

Prayer: Lord, let me look to you for strength to forgive myself and others. May I be willing to give others second chances, just as you have done for me.

Blessed is she who understands that God gives second chances, for she shall walk free from judgment.

Day 12

And God said, "Let the water under the sky be gathered to one place, and let dry ground appear. And it was so."

GENESIS 1:9

In the Twinkling of an Eye

NO ALARM JARRED me from the luxury of lying in bed, listening to the sounds of the surf and praying. Though my brain had been awake for an hour, my body still hadn't moved. It lingered, even though my mind prompted, "It's time to get up. It's time to check the tide."

"Nope," my mind countered, "There's no hurry."

I pondered why I wouldn't get up and thought about what usually convinced me to get up on non-alarm days. I would rise when the needs of my body, for food, for the bathroom, or just to move, spoke more loudly than the comfort of the bed.

This reminds me of spiritual steppingstones. God speaks to me about an issue that needs to change. I pray for days, or weeks or years, and little or nothing changes. Then one day, literally in an instant, during prayer or worship there's a permanent transition. I feel the difference on the inside, and it lasts.

What makes that moment different? It's a supernatural moment when the God of the universe enters the equation in an active way and speaks. Just as he spoke at creation, he now declares, "It's time." I've heard it described like this: "It sometimes takes a long time for God to act suddenly." God promised Abraham descendants as numerous as the stars in the sky (Genesis 25:4), but no son came forth—not even a daughter. Abraham and Sarah grew too old to have a child. "Then suddenly, one day" strangers happened by and prophesied that within a year Sarah would deliver a child. She conceived, and the prophecy was fulfilled.

Israel waited hundreds of years for the Messiah. "Then suddenly one day" an angel appeared to Mary. Nine months later Jesus arrived.

When and why does the "suddenly" moment finally happen? When does God speak forth transformation? When he knows that everything is in place with regard to his perfect timing. His child is ready. History is in the right place. Supporting factors are aligned. Then he moves, as he did in creation, and something new is born.

The moment of salvation works like that. There's a supernatural element whereby the God of the universe transcends humanity and transacts an eternal change in us. We can pray and push, but until God knows everything is right, we wait.

If you've ever experienced one of those moments, you know what I mean. There's an indescribable, undeniable change that happens within the space of a heartbeat. An indelible point of demarcation is reached, and the change lasts till death, and maybe into eternity.

One of the most vivid of such times for me resulted in the healing of my childhood sense of rejection. "When I was pregnant with you, we couldn't afford to have another baby along with the two we already had," my mother said "so I convinced myself you were a tumor."

My six-year-old brain froze as it processed my mother's words. *Is that why I don't have a baby book, and my brother and sister do?* Throughout the years my mom somehow thought that dubbing me her little tumor was an endearment. To me the image screamed, "Unwanted. Unloved."

Three or four years later my inebriated mom staggered into the living room and slurred, "I'm kicking you out of the house." When she'd forced my older brother and sister to leave together an hour earlier, they thought I was safe, so they hadn't waited for me.

"I'm going to make you leave after dark, and don't you dare go to your dad" (who was working a thirty-minute walk away). "I hope you get molested." Though terrified, I made it safely to my dad, despite what she had said. My brother and sister were also safe.

After receiving Jesus at age seventeen, I prayed continually for healing of that wound. By the time mom died when I was thirty-five, I knew in my head that my mom loved me, but my emotions never moved past the words of rejection.

Twenty years later God healed me. At a retreat a prayer leader placed her hand on me and prayed for God to pull out the root of rejection. In an instant the sense of rejection left me, and I have never been plagued with it again, not even for a moment. I know inside and out that my mom loved me.

A stronghold of fear also flourished in my life, starting in childhood. Once fear begins in one facet of our life, it easily spreads to other areas. For me, I feared any injury would result in lasting damage.

When I injured my shoulder as an older adult, I panicked. I prayed fervently for the fear to depart.

One day, during a seemingly ordinary quiet time, I prayed . . . and the fear left me—instantly. Now I could say in faith, "Quit your whining, shoulder (or ankle or whatever hurt), and do your job. You are fine." The fear-induced pain would stop.

I know that God is capable of doing, and willing to do, the same for you, even in problem areas for which you have seen no answer for years. No obstacle is too great for him.

> "*I am the* LORD: *in its time I will do this swiftly.*"
> ISAIAH 60:22

Prayer: Lord, may I be faithful in prayer and belief, knowing that at any moment you can either totally change any situation or reshape me.

Blessed is the person who realizes that it can take a long time for a "suddenly" to happen, for she shall understand that God can bring transformation in the twinkling of an eye.

Day 13

Jesus said, "Let the little children come to me, and do not hinder them, for the kingdom of heaven belongs to such as these."

MATTHEW 19:14

Merriment

FROLICKING IN THE sand and surf, the dogs caught my eye. Their exuberance stopped me, and I simply watched. They would hunker down and then rush at each other with mouths open to pretend to attack each other. Seeming to laugh with uninhibited joy, they repeated their antics over and over—dashing circles around their owners, who chatted on the beach. My own grin stretched as widely as theirs.

In fact, my heart swelled with joy so great it made me want to run and play with the same carefree abandon; to overcome limitations of age and not to care what others thought. Eventually the owners parted and strolled away, but not before the dogs had marked my heart (in a different way from their usual marking of territory).

I believe that this scene reflects what God wants to restore in us. I usually think of Adam and Eve as having been serious in their work before being filled with shame over their disobedience. But let's rethink that. Try to imagine perfection: perfect climate, perfect mate, perfect times with God.

If I were Eve, I'd have been playing tag and teasing Adam that he couldn't catch me. Maybe I'd have played a game of hide and seek or tried to ride one of the animals. I'd have run full speed and rolled down a grassy hill the way a child delights to do. I'd have laughed, giggled, and played.

After all, peer pressure didn't exist, so there could have been no worries about what someone else might have thought. Joy reigned in the Garden of Eden: joy in playing, in working, and in the beauty surrounding Adam and Eve. Hanging out with the Creator brought the greatest joy of all.

At festivals and on other momentous occasions, the Israelites danced, sang, and played the timbrels. They knew how to celebrate with all that was within them. We read in Exodus 15:20, "Then Miriam . . . took a timbrel in her hand, and all the women followed her, with timbrels and dancing." Can you just picture such unrestrained elation?

The exuberant play of the dogs struck a chord in my heart because I used to play with the same abandon. I learned it from my dad. In spite of the painful moments my early life had offered, he always found a reason to celebrate the simple pleasures. I remember opening the refrigerator in high school to find a silly face, along with a love note to my stepmom, drawn on the butcher wrap of the lunch meat. Sometimes his silliness got a little too silly, and I would roll my adolescent eyes.

A sense of humor and playfulness was valued by my dad, and I knew it was safe to be me around him even if other areas of life didn't feel safe. The loss of playfulness years later symbolized the loss of my belief that my life was predictable and secure; that I was not valued and needed to become someone else.

As an elementary school teacher, I loved providing experiences that would make my students laugh out loud. Seeing them smile made my day. My goal was to provide a safe learning environment, and their laughter proved to me that they felt safe. What I didn't recognize till recently was how safe I had felt joking and being silly with them, because I knew they valued it—even the older students.

The same held true for me as a mom. To the best of my ability, I created adventures for my daughters. We ate green pancakes on St. Patrick's Day and peanut butter bees for snacks. We built forts and played chase. When they were teens we danced around the house and sang silly songs. Even my older daughter, who didn't tend toward silliness, once gave the Thanksgiving turkey a name (Bertha), along with an oil massage, and danced around the kitchen with it before putting it in the oven.

I felt safe doing those activities with my children, and later with my three grandsons. I knew they enjoyed them as much as I did. In fact, I got double pleasure because it was so much fun to watch them.

The playfulness did not emerge, however, wherever and whenever I didn't feel safe. My job situation changed right at the point when my daughters left for college. I became a reading teacher with students from K–5 moving through my room every 30–45 minutes, instead of working with twenty to thirty students of my own all day. They received small group instruction from six to eight educational assistants and me. My job was to implement a mandated curriculum "correctly" and mentor the EAs to do the same. School became serious work with little leeway for playfulness.

God had been brilliant to take me far away to Myrtle Beach for my time of reprieve. He knew I'd likely never see any of those people again, so it felt safe to begin to be me again. I didn't care if they rolled their eyes or judged me. He had created me with a silly streak, and it no doubt gives him pleasure to see my heart open up, just as it gives me pleasure to see others having fun. What better place than the beach to reinforce for me that, with him, it's always safe to be me.

Whether the real you exudes joy in quiet or noisy ways, God wants you to see his love note in the refrigerator. He wants your smile to light up with reciprocal love for him. He wants your joy to cause you to feel free to frolic with the same jubilation as the dogs on the beach, even if just on the inside. He is always safe. The greatest joy is hanging out with him.

I praise you because I am fearfully and wonderfully made;
your works are wonderful, I know that full well.
PSALM 139:14

Prayer: Almighty God, may I know that you are my safe place. With you I am free to be who you created me to be.

Blessed is the one who gains pleasure from watching
playful animals, for her joy will return.

Day 14

I will give you a new heart and put a new spirit in you; I will remove from you your heart of stone and give you a heart of flesh.

EZEKIEL 36:26

Sand Castles

SPRING BREAK FAMILIES, including my daughter and grandson, filled the beach during my third week in Myrtle Beach. My grandson and I enjoyed people-watching as we strolled along the shoreline. Laughter erupted from volleyball games and swimmers. Dogs chased frisbees and sticks. Moms sat under sun umbrellas, while youngsters dug in the sand nearby.

We walked past an ornate sand castle standing on the beach. Two teens were putting finishing touches on the majestic structure while we watched. Earlier that day we had tried, and failed, to do the same. Each time we had carefully emptied our bucket, the sand had crumbled into a shapeless mess.

Our curiosity gave us the courage to ask, "How do you get the sand to slide out of the bucket without falling apart?"

"You need to have enough moisture in the sand. If it's too dry it will fall apart. But if it's too wet it will collapse. You'll get a feel for it. Keep trying, and you'll find the right mixture."

We experimented with different amounts of water, but our sand still fell apart. We gave up and went looking for shells instead. I left the beach that afternoon realizing that, though I would never likely be a sand-castle master, I was a super sleuth when it came to shells.

Wait. Shouldn't I have persevered with regard to water levels until I got the consistency of that sand perfect? What kind of person walks away in failure? How could I respect myself if I didn't learn the art of sand-castle building, especially with my grandson.

In my younger years I would have done just that. I would have asked for more advice, watched people, and tried over and over until I could do it just right. I also would have been exhausted and cried a bunch of tears over something that would never matter.

My children taught me that not everything in life has to be perfect and that I don't have to be good at everything. When they were teens they liked to have friends come to our house after Sunday night youth group. At first, I stressed and wore myself out making sure the house was immaculate. If it wasn't, I fussed aloud. I fussed about whether the food was good enough. Finally, they said, "Mom. Relax. Our friends don't care if the house is clean or the food is gourmet. They want a place to be where they feel loved. You make them feel loved."

Huh? I did want the teens to feel loved. I didn't realize that they just wanted me to see them, listen to them, and be there with an open home and open heart. Isn't this essentially what we want from God—to be seen, heard, acknowledged, and loved.

It took a couple of years, but I did learn that lesson. A different situation with my daughter reinforced it in my brain. Although she was an honor student who loved learning, as a senior her calculus class stressed her out. She approached me about dropping the class. As we discussed it I shared that I hadn't taken calculus in high school or college and had never needed it. Based on her longer-term interests, we concluded that she likely would never need it, either. She dropped the class with my blessing.

That didn't make her math teacher happy: "You'll regret not finishing calculus." He made her feel as if her life would be ruined if she didn't continue. We stood firm, and instead she got an internship at the local newspaper, which led to her becoming an editor on the college newspaper. She has never needed higher math in her career field, but has required honed writing skills.

The point in both situations is that none of us has the time or energy or interest to accomplish everything. We need to prioritize what's truly important to us. Being fresh to hang out with teenagers was more important for me than maintaining a perfect house. Learning about newspapers was more important for my daughter than being frustrated over advanced math skills that wouldn't be utilized in life.

In Acts, the Grecian Jews complained against the Hebraic Jews that their widows were being overlooked in the daily distribution of food. "So, the Twelve gathered all the disciples together and said, 'It would not be right for us to neglect the ministry of the word of God in order to wait on tables'" (Acts 6:2). The Twelve asked the larger group to find godly men who could be trusted with that responsibility.

I will confess, however, that a few years before coming to Myrtle Beach, I tried to prove my value to someone by taking on more and more responsibility, to the point of exhaustion. The sand castle made me realize that the same dynamic applied to people pleasing. It took so much time and energy that I had few reserves left for the activities God was asking me to do.

I'm pretty certain you face the same dilemma in your life. You have too much to do, and even one small added task can push you to becoming overwhelmed. My advice here isn't deep or profound. It isn't even unique or different. You've heard it before, but let me say it this way to remind you of what you already know. Would you rather:

- wear yourself out getting sand to release properly from a bucket, or find shells with someone you love?
- present a perfect house, or have the energy to open your heart to others?

> *"Seek first his kingdom and his righteousness, and all these things will be given to you as well."*
> MATTHEW 6:33

Prayer: God, direct my time and energy to align with the love I have for you. Help me trust that your adventures will work out for me much better than my attempts at people pleasing.

Blessed are those who learn to enjoy finding shells, for they shall have time for God.

Day 15

Jesus Christ is the same yesterday and today and forever.

HEBREWS 13:8

Who Moved?

COLD WIND WHIPPED as I pulled my jacket tighter. Shivering, I wished for the sun to come back out from behind the clouds. "Why won't you just stay out? You make my body relax with your warmth. It's not fun on the beach without you."

"Wait." I paused with the kind of realization that will make you go, "Oh, duh." You see, I kept thinking from the perspective of the sun moving, when in reality it was the cloud bank that moved. Those clouds floated in front of it and then away. They were the culprits that made me wish for more layers of clothing. The sun remained stable.

The *aha* moment continued. I thought about how, in our lives, God remains stable. He doesn't move. Now, while that sounds obvious, do we always think that way? Or do we cry out, "God, where are you? Why can't I hear you? Why do you feel so far away?" We've likely all heard a pastor say, "If someone moved, it's you." But somehow the concrete example before me cemented the concept in my understanding.

Yet, while it's true that we may have moved, it's not always ourselves who obstruct our view of God. Sometimes oppression from our enemy snakes its way across our vision and settles around our life. Sometimes trauma strikes like a sudden storm cloud so black it obliterates everything in the sky.

What do we do when darkness clouds our vision? May I suggest a two-part strategy? First, figure out what is obscuring your view of God and then seek him, asking what to do about the problem. If we don't know what the obstacle is, we can ask. James 1:5 tells us that if we lack wisdom, God will give it to us. If the obstruction is about you, seek forgiveness and watch the block dissolve instantly. If it's not you, ask God to fight for you and bring you back into the fullness of his warmth and light.

Sometimes we have sin standing between God and us. Ouch. I remember the bitter anger I stuffed inside as I put on my "Oh, I'm fine" face for church friends. But the anger caused my focus to linger on the problem instead of on the One who loves me. I was mired in the circumstances instead of immersing myself in my Healer. My normal worship and prayer times became lifeless, distracted as I was by ignoble thoughts. A trusted friend who knew the story of the pain behind my anger, listened to me relate the facts and then quietly asked me, "How's your heart?"

The arrow hit home. Later, in the privacy of my room, tears fell as God simultaneously broke my heart with the reality of my sin and held me in his healing arms while I asked forgiveness. Just as the sun breaks through clouds with glorious light, so also the glory of God filled my spirit and soul. With my heart cleansed, I was able to authentically pray for the one who had caused me pain.

Sometimes the voice of the accuser screams in our heads so loudly that we can't hear the truth. "You're a fake. You'll never measure up. If people knew the real you, they'd drop you instantly. They're not friends. They are just being nice because they have to."

To greater and lesser degrees, we have all heard that voice. Its persistence and volume demand our attention. When we bow in agreement, the voice gets more strident. If we fight it with a scripture that speaks the opposite truth (you are loved, you belong, your past is forgiven), however, we resist the enemy, and he will flee (James 4:7). Sometimes this is not instantaneous, so we need to persevere in our declaration.

I love this verse: "The Lord your God is with you; the Mighty Warrior who saves. He will take great delight in you; in his love he will no longer rebuke you, will rejoice over you with singing" (Zephaniah 3:17). We can declare this verse over ourselves or ask others to pray for us until we are strong enough to do so.

Trauma from betrayal, the death of a loved one, injury or illness, or worse, can strike like a sudden thunder and lightning storm. The sounds, the sights, the hair plastered to our heads dripping into our face, cause us to race away to shelter. We can choose the false shelter of withdrawing and hiding from the world and God. Or we can choose the shelter of the Almighty God. When we can't see the sun, we still know it's in the sky. Likewise, God never leaves. We can throw ourselves into his comforting arms until the storm passes. For a time we may need to walk by faith, not by sight, until the sight returns.

The day after my *aha* moment, scattered clouds filled the sky again. This time I wore a skin-tight base layer, a long-sleeved tee, a sweater, and a hooded jacket. My preparation kept me warm when the clouds flitted in front of my friend, the sun. In the same way I can layer worship, prayer, the Word, and confession of known sin to protect me from the blasts of arctic air from the enemy.

I choose to remember that God is faithful. He opens my eyes to sin, speaks truth until oppression passes by, and will send his warrior angels to fight for me. When trauma lessens, I will realize that he has walked with me through the darkest storm and brought healing to my soul.

> "Because he loves me," says the LORD, "I will rescue him."
> PSALM 91:14

Prayer: Heavenly Father, thank you that I can dwell in the shelter of the Most High and rest in the shadow of the Almighty. I can say that you are my refuge and my fortress, my God in whom I trust.

Blessed is she who knows that the sun is stable, for she shall see the stable Son.

Day 16

"Then young women will dance and be glad, young men and old as well. I will turn their mourning into gladness."

JEREMIAH 31:13

Beware the Spies

MY EXCITEMENT GREW with each step as I ventured up the ramp to the dolphin cruise. Grinning, I settled into a seat just below the captain's cabin. After a few friendly words to the passenger next to me, it became obvious that he didn't want to visit, so I leaned back to enjoy the adventure.

Despite my earlier private dolphin show, the dolphin cruise piqued my interest with its potential for allowing me to see a whole pod of dolphins and the prospect of a boat ride down the serene river waterway.

"Folks, it's possible to stay on this intracoastal waterway all the way from Boston to Florida without ever venturing out into the ocean." This intriguing statement from the captain fed my imagination during the slow trek through a crowded part of our route. *Hmm*, I mused. *A route that bad guys could use to escape detection.*

Actual scene: Seagulls circled the boat, mewing loudly. They hovered closely for miles. A grandmother stumbled forward to sit on the step that led to the front deck.

"Are you allowed to sit there, Grandma?" asked a young boy and girl who followed her.

"I don't know, but I'm going to sit here anyway."

She stared pensively out at the waterway and the mansions lining the shore. The brisk wind prompted her grandson to burrow close to her side. To our right a young man and his girlfriend moved from their seat to stand at the rail, moving back to their seats when the wind picked up.

My imagination had embarked on a river ride all its own: Mansions of the rich, famous, and criminal lined the shores of the waterway, impressive in their simple elegance. Cupolas with telescopes perched atop many of them. Lawns and ornate pathways led to docks: a picture of serenity.

Yet, woven deeply within one mansion, deception and intrigue hid in secret chambers. The safety of a nation hung in the balance. Agent GD, also known as Grandma Dorsey, strategically posed as a tourist on the dolphin cruise. PHON (Please Help Our Nation) Intelligence had tracked the path of the known terrorist Dante Spumoni to a location somewhere on the intracoastal waterway near Myrtle Beach, South Carolina. The Hawkson Diamond, lost in a museum heist, would provide the final piece in his weapon of mass destruction. The Ditonium Splitsodian would split the earth in half, while Dante escaped to Mars in his space rocket.

Agent GD needed to intercept the diamond before the exchange could take place and then alert her team to the location of the Ditonium Splitsodian so it could be destroyed. Aware of every movement, she surreptitiously eyed another grandma sitting on the step leading to the front of the boat. Was she hiding from the birds overhead? Agent GD had already figured out that these were drones spying on the boat, which meant that Dante believed the diamond was aboard.

The young man and his girlfriend presented youth and agility that could facilitate a quick getaway once an exchange was made. Was their move to the railing a signal that they were in place?

How would Agent GD determine which one had the diamond?

"Ladies and gentlemen, we are stopping near the drawbridge and moving over to allow smaller boats to pass by. Once the bridge opens, we will be on our way again and will be able to pick up speed. Thank you for your patience."

Suddenly, Agent GD jumped up on her seat, grabbed the captain's hat, and ripped out the lining. She grasped the diamond and secretly slipped it into the hand of the young man. While GD radioed her team, the man and his girlfriend slid over the side of the boat into a waiting small craft. They sped off so quickly that the scrambling bad guys had no hope of catching them.

Agent GD's team breached the doors of a nearby mansion and blew up the Ditonium Splitsodian. Meanwhile, another team swarmed the dolphin cruise, handcuffed the captain, and put a new pilot in place.

"You did it again, Agent GD. How did you figure it out?"

"I noticed that the grandma's bag was filled with snacks and that she wore a knee brace under her pants. I knew she couldn't move quickly enough to make an exchange and was able at least to eliminate her as a suspect. It was suspicious, though, that our boat needed to move to the side. So, I quickly scanned the area. One nearby mansion had the same DS logo as the captain's hat. I knew then that he was connected to the crime ring. The only logical place for the diamond was his hat."

"But how did you know the young couple were good guys?"

"Oh, that was easy. When the man turned around, he winked and tugged his hair. That signal is one my grandson and I used when he was little and we played 'find me when I'm disguised.' I knew immediately it was him."

I bet you are wondering what the point of this story is. Mostly it's just for fun. God gave us humor and imaginations, so let's use them. I inwardly laughed during the whole cruise as my mini drama played out in my head.

Second, this anecdote can help us remember that God also gave us the Holy Spirit and his Word to discern good and evil and to give us guidance. Agent GD's ears and mind stayed tuned to every little clue, just as our ears and spirit can stay tuned to every clue from God.

PS We saw only one faraway dolphin on the cruise.

> *"When he, the Spirit of truth, comes, he
> will guide you into all the truth."*
> JOHN 16:13

Prayer: God, restore the humor and imagination you created in us. It's part of the childlike wonder you welcome. If ours seem lost, show us where these qualities are hidden within.

*Blessed are those who see with the eyes of a child, for
they shall be filled with laughter and joy.*

Day 17

*The LORD is close to the brokenhearted
and saves those who are crushed in spirit.*

PSALM 34:18

Beauty Revealed

MY STEP QUICKENED on the path to the beach. Eagerness for my morning trek for treasure filled me. Never disappointing, the beach beckoned, and with full abandon I raised my face in praise to God. In overflowing gratitude I acknowledged the many gifts, both physical and spiritual, that he had already hand-delivered to me.

My eyes were searching the sand in anticipation of new discoveries when a whelk shell captured my attention. Seeing its brokenness, I walked right on by, but a sudden thought turned me around, and I picked it up. Examining every side, I realized that I was seeing something new. With the outer casing broken away, I could see the beauty inside. A graceful spiral spanned from the fully intact crown to the tip.

I'll bet that you instantly see the analogy here. Our brokenness can bring forth our inner beauty. But let's take it a bit deeper than that. The outer wall that broke off my shell had grown thick, almost like a callous that protects our hands when we overwork them. It makes me wonder about the thick walls we put up that God needs to break away. We choose from a variety of them:

- The smiling mask wall. "I'm good. Everything is going great."
- The withdraw from everyone and make excuses about being busy wall.
- The wall of hostility that spews angry barbs and sarcasm.
- The "I'm too cool for you" wall.

Pain throws up walls. If the wound is addressed right away, those walls are temporary and tumble down easily. Injury acknowledged by love digs out the root before it grows and nurtures us back to health.

But when pain isn't seen and isn't heard, we fortify the wall by becoming expert builders, choosing one of these building materials:

1. A hedge that looks pretty but grows long barbs ready to jab anyone who gets too close. While the spikes are intended for the one inflicting pain, innocent people often get pricked.
2. The wooden fence. While sturdy with its posts, crossbars, and slats, this wall could be easily broken down. We use it when we secretly hope someone will notice us and breach the wall to save us.
3. The brick-and-mortar wall. Much sturdier than the wooden fence, this effective barrier intimidates the faint-hearted, thus serving its purpose. Only the truly courageous will find a ladder and scale the edifice to find us.
4. The chain link barbed wire fence. While others can see us, they can't get to us. If they scale the wall or attempt to cut through the wire, we are ready with our water balloons or basketball to hurl at them. Our determination scares away those who see our pain and want to help.

Our walls keep others out, and they also keep us in. They trap us like victims unable to escape. Our situation paralyzes us, and we see no way out. But God always has a way out.

"He himself is our peace, who has made the two groups one and has destroyed the barrier, the dividing wall of hostility, by setting aside in his flesh the law with its commands and regulations. His purpose was to create in himself one new humanity out of the two, thus making peace, and in one body to reconcile both of them to God through the cross, by which he put to death their hostility" (Ephesians 2:14–16).

While this passage speaks about Jews and Gentiles, I have often prayed it over troubled relationships. Our God is well able to destroy the dividing wall of hostility between us and someone else. Even if the other person remains hostile, he can eradicate the hostility in us.

After years of my seeing no apparent change in one relationship, God opened my eyes. I saw that, while I had prayed many times to forgive and had repented of my bitterness, the continued offenses piled on to the point that I had been praying the words while my heart no longer meant them. That is, until God set aside this special time and place to wash away my defenses with his love.

After returning to Arizona, I adapted a strategy from Lysa Terkeurst's book *Forgiving What You Can't Forget*. I typed a list of every offense I could think of, no matter how long ago the incident had taken place or how many times I claimed to have forgiven it. Then I prayed over each issue individually: "Lord, I choose to forgive _____ for _____. Whatever my emotions can't let go of yet, I place under the blood of Jesus." I highlighted that offense in red to represent the reality that his blood had covered it. I repeated the process until all were highlighted.

It took three days, as my heart couldn't address very many at a time. But when I was finished I felt light and free. This person and I now are better friends than we had been in many years. We enjoy spending time together. My prickly hedge no longer jabs them, and they respond with respect. In other words, my change led to their change.

God broke down my thick wall so that the beauty of his grace inside could be seen once again.

> *My sacrifice, O God, is a broken spirit; a broken*
> *and contrite heart you, God, will not despise.*
> PSALM 51:17

Prayer: Gentle Shepherd, may I allow you to break off any hard walls around my heart. Open up the beauty that you have placed within me.

> *Blessed is the person who finds beauty in brokenness,*
> *for God will uncover their own beauty.*

Day 18

I rejoice in your word like one who discovers a great treasure.
PSALM 119:162 NLT

Debris Field

PEOPLE, DOGS, BIRDS, waves, shells, houses, signs. With so much vying for my attention, I almost overlooked a most important part of the beach—the debris field. Patches of shattered shells dotted the sand.

Previously, my eyes had landed only on the whole shells scattered everywhere. Today I knelt at one of the debris fields, hoping for great discoveries. It did not disappoint. Mixed in with the fragments I found whole shells, both hidden and protected by the larger, broken pieces—majestic perfection so tiny that three or four of these delicate wonders fit on my pinkie fingernail.

When I thought I'd investigated everything, I moved to a different side of the patch, only to discover completely new treasures I hadn't noticed before. Finished, I walked on down the beach, but on the way back I stopped again—and found shells I had missed earlier. Some waited, uncovered, right in plain sight.

The same kind of blindness happens when I read the Bible. I can read the same book 67 times and, upon reading #68, see truths I had missed before. Sometimes particular spiritual truths go unnoticed because so many other spiritual truths, like the seashells in a debris field, are vying for my attention. At other times new understandings arise only after my connecting one passage to another. Frequently, especially when I'm drawing information from the Old Testament to better understand the New, learning more about Jewish history and culture reveals a deeper understanding of our Christian faith.

Psalm 22, a known Messianic psalm, falls into the last category. In verse 6, "I am a worm and not a man," God left a hidden picture for discovery by those of us a long way removed from the original language.

Tôlā, the Hebrew word used here, indicates a particular worm called the crimson worm. When the female tola is ready to lay eggs, she climbs up a tree and permanently attaches herself to its trunk. Once she's affixed, it's physically impossible for her to detach from the tree without being ripped apart.

She then forms a hard, protective shell around her body and lays her eggs within it. After the eggs hatch, the mother sacrifices her life for her children as they feed on her body for several days (some say three). When the mother dies, she secretes a crimson fluid, staining both the tree and the larvae. For the rest of their life they will remain crimson colored—thus the name of the worm. After her death the hard shell decays to a white, waxy substance that looks like a puff of wool on the tree. The tail of the worm tucks up to the head and forms a heart before falling like snow to the ground (Henry Morris, *Biblical Basis for Modern Science*).

In the female tola worm life cycle we clearly see the gospel message. First Peter 2:24 says that Jesus "himself bore our sins in his body on the cross." Jesus willingly allowed himself to be attached to the tree (the cross), not coming down until he had sacrificed his life for us.

Spiritually, we feed on the body of Jesus as we accept his substitutionary death for us. During the Feast of Tabernacles Jesus declared, "I am the bread of life. Your ancestors ate the manna in the wilderness, yet they died. But here is the bread that comes down from heaven, which anyone may eat and not die. I am the living bread that came down from heaven. Whoever eats this bread will live forever. This bread is my flesh, which I will give for the life of the world" (John 6:48–51).

There's no escaping the crimson stain as a symbol of the blood of Jesus: "the blood of Jesus, [God's] Son, purifies us from all sin" (1 John 1:7). And the white, wool-like substance around the female tola worm gives us deeper insight into Isaiah 1:18: "'Come now, let us settle the matter,' says the LORD. 'Though your sins are like scarlet, they shall be as white as snow; though they are red as crimson, they shall be like wool.'" Though different Hebrew words are used for scarlet and crimson, both refer in Isaiah's image to the tola worm.

The Old Testament connection to the tola worm looks ahead to the story of Jesus in other ways, as well. People crushed the dried remains of this worm to make scarlet dye. Scarlet yarn was used, along with blue yarn, purple yarn, and finely twisted linen to fashion the curtains of the tabernacle, including between the Holy Place and the Most Holy Place. It's this curtain that tore in two from the top to the bottom when Jesus died. Scarlet yarn was also used in the ephod and the breast piece worn by the high priests as they came before God on behalf of the people.

In building the tabernacle, God instructed Moses to layer four different coverings over the top. One of those layers consisted of ram skins dyed red. The Hebrew word for red here doesn't specify that the tola worm was used, but it makes me wonder. If that is indeed the case, it presents an amazing picture of the tent, where God met with his people, being covered by the blood of Jesus.

Both in Old Testament times and still today, the remains of this worm were/are used to make a medicine that helps the heart beat smoothly. "Let not your hearts be troubled," says Jesus in John 14:1. Could this constitute an incredible embedded message, spoken hundreds of years before the birth of Christ?

> *If you look for it as for silver and search for it as for hidden treasure, then you will understand the fear of the LORD and find the knowledge of God.*
> PROVERBS 2:4–5

Prayer: Heavenly Father, give me a hunger to find deeply embedded truth in your Word.

Blessed is the person who looks carefully at broken pieces, for they will discover more than they ever dreamed.

Day 19

You will shine [in a warped and crooked generation] like stars in the sky as you hold firmly to the word of life.

PHILIPPIANS 2:15

Shiny

IN THE WET sand broken bits of shells stuck in yet another debris field caught my eye as they glistened in the sun. One would think that broken pieces wouldn't be good for anything—except maybe for snagging tiny shells like the ones we talked about in Day 18. However, these were so beautiful in themselves that a creative idea formed in my mind. What if, when I got back home, I put a layer of the crushed shells down as a ground cover in a small area of my garden. Maybe they would set off the beauty of the intact shells I also planned to display there.

That day I filled my bucket to the brim with handfuls from the debris field. I continued the next day, and the next, until upon my return to the condo two small boxes on the balcony held a three-inch layer. Then I experimented with some whole shells on top to see the effect and got excited at how perfectly the background drew attention to them.

After sitting on the balcony for a while, my crushed and tiny shells dried out and no longer glittered, so they wouldn't catch anyone's eye. Soaking them in water would replenish the shine, but soon they would dry out again. I tried rubbing them with oil—and it worked! Long-lasting sparkle returned.

Regardless of whether the shells were whole or crushed, it was the glossiness that transformed them. Even the larger, whole shells remained dull without moisture from either water or the oil (with the exception of olive shells, which always have a natural shine to them). On the beach, when the shattered shells remained wet, they seemed to shout, "Come and see. Find out why I am magnificent, despite the fact that I am broken." That's why they had caught my eye.

We can cry out in the same way: "How am I still beautiful despite the fact that life situations have crushed me? Come and see." Our reason is the same. We have water and oil that make us shine. Our water comes from the One who told the Samaritan woman at the well that, if she knew to whom she was speaking, she would ask him for living water (John 4:10). Our oil comes from the Holy Spirit, who dwells within us if we know Jesus as Savior.

That all sounds really good. But in practical terms, what does it even look like? How do we start? How do we get to that place?

The process starts with God looking down and seeing a heart, buried in all the chaos and rubble of life, that loves him. A smile forms in his heart and on his face as he sends a special little gift, maybe a particular seashell we've always wanted. We recognize it for what it is: God declaring, "I know you. I see you." Our heart is so touched that praise and adoration well up within us and escape from our mouth as we see past the pain to Abba (Daddy God).

He does it again. Maybe this time it's a song, or a verse like Jeremiah 31:4: "I will build you up again, and you, Virgin Israel [insert your name] will be rebuilt. Again you will take up your timbrels and go out to dance with the joyful." We recognize his special touch again and respond with a grateful spirit. (The key is recognizing the gifts, because they are what draws our attention to him.)

He doesn't look at us with disgust or disappointment or judgment. Instead, Abba sees the beauty of the ones he created. When we are free from the fear of judgment, shame, and reprisal, our hearts blossom. Our faces become radiant. He choreographs a dance for us. All we need to do is accept his invitation and step confidently, knowing that every movement was specially designed for us by the One who knows us better than we know ourselves.

All of this happens through the work of the Holy Spirit. It's fascinating. Just as the shells needed either water or oil to stay shiny, so the Holy Spirit is likened to both water and oil.

This realization makes me ponder what draws our attention to God, which causes me to think about what draws me to other people. That's easy. Regardless of whether they are gregarious or shy, I am attracted to those who show love to others. Their kindness and patience make me feel safe. A peaceful serenity emanates from them. Joy trickles out as they speak. Their gentle speech reveals wholesomeness, and self-control is evident.

You've probably noticed that those qualities sound like the fruit of the Spirit (Galatians 5:22–23). I noticed this as I wrote them out, although I hadn't started out with that connection in mind. I had just thought about what makes me want to be around certain people. Even if they have only one or two of those traits, I like to be with them. I think my question got answered: when the fruit of the Spirit begins to grow in me, then others will see it and see God reflected.

So rejoice, you crushed shell, for you will reflect the glory of the One who created you and builds you up continually. You are an element in the debris field, and he is the beautiful shell. Your shout will catch the eyes and ears of others as you declare, "Look at the magnificent One, the One who gives me life. Let us dance with him. Let's move at the sound of God's voice. Let's partner in this season on the earth with the Creator of all things."

> *May the God of hope fill you with all joy and peace*
> *as you trust in him, so that you may overflow*
> *with hope in the power of the Holy Spirit.*
> ROMANS 15:13

Prayer: Thank you, God, that you use the crushed places in my life to bring forth new beauty. May I choose to see the good that you bring out of tough situations, and may you be glorified.

Blessed is the one who sees beauty in shattered shells,
for she shall understand the dance of the Savior.

Day 20

When he was at the table with them, he took bread, gave thanks, broke it and began to give it to them. Then their eyes were opened and they recognized him, and he disappeared from their sight. They asked each other, "Were not our hearts burning within us while he talked with us on the road and opened the Scriptures to us?"

LUKE 24:30–32

You'll Know It When You See It

"Hi," I SAID, passing a fellow beachcomber. "Any treasures?"

"I found three shark teeth." He pulled out a small container and showed me three tiny fossilized black teeth.

"Shark teeth?"

"Yes. I found six yesterday."

"With all the broken bits of black shells, how do you know when it's a shark tooth?"

"Shark teeth are shiny. You'll know one when you see it."

Over the following days I chatted with different people and discovered that the majority of searchers on the beach sought shark teeth. Whenever I asked for more guidance on finding one myself, the response was the same: "They are shiny. You'll know it when you see one."

I searched hard each day. I found chips of black shells but no shark teeth. "Lord, would you lead me to a shark tooth? I want to give one to my grandson." By the time he arrived for spring break, I still hadn't found one, despite having searched for days.

The afternoon after he arrived I was showing him the shells on my balcony when a sudden thought struck me. The beachcombers had been looking for the shark teeth at low tide in the debris fields.

I grabbed my previously gathered broken bits and began to sift through them. Sure enough, in the second handful I found a perfect shark tooth. I recognized it the instant I saw it, just as the people had said I would. I laughed. Once again, God had sent a personalized blessing.

I have talked about hearing God speak to me. I will confess, that I sometimes wonder which voices are my own and which are truly from God. Here are some ways I discern the difference.

I love the comments of the two men walking to Emmaus. "Did not our hearts burn within us?" they marveled (Matthew 24:13–32). When we experience God's nearness, our stirred hearts feel full. Remember shalom? A sense of holiness and completeness matching what scholars define as shalom infuses us, so that we feel satiated with wholeness, completeness, and peace. The exhilaration is exciting and calming at the same time. In Ephesians Paul talks about the church, "which is his body, the fullness of him who *fills everything* in every way" (1:23, emphasis mine).

The Holy Spirit is our connection to God. It's through him that we experience God's presence. He indwells us in the same way our own spirit lives within us.

I came to know Jesus as my Savior at seventeen at a Bible club meeting but became fearful of the Holy Spirit when controversy broke out over the gift of tongues. I was so confused and remember saying, "God, I don't know enough about the Bible to know who is right and who is wrong. I am going to put it on the shelf, and when I know more I will take it back down and figure out what's true." Twenty years passed. Sadly, I put all of the Holy Spirit on the shelf not just the controversial part. Twenty years passed. Sadly, I put all of the Holy Spirit on the shelf, not just the controversial part.

Then one summer my daughters and I went on a two-week mission trip. Daily, I heard other leaders say, "I was praying about ___, and God said ___." I kept thinking, *I've prayed and read my Bible every morning, and God hasn't spoken to me.*

Shortly after, a new staff member at school shared about having prayed over her students' desks each morning at her previous job. One day she sensed God telling her a student was planning to commit suicide. She confronted him privately, and he confessed his plan to kill himself that afternoon. She talked with him, loved him, and got help for him. Because she heard God speak, his life was saved that day.

The following Sunday night after church, I sat alone in my car and prayed, "God, it's obvious people are hearing you through the Holy Spirit. I don't want to be afraid of the Holy Spirit anymore."

Instantly, I heard God's voice in my mind. "Oh, good, now that you're ready to listen, I have lots to say." Before that I heard from sermons, reading the Bible or devotional books. After that I began to hear his voice (in my mind) when I worshiped, prayed, and lived life.

How did I know the voice was his and not the enemy's? That's a good question, since the Bible alerts us that Satan disguises himself as an angel of light (2 Corinthians 11:14). We already talked about the burning in our heart, but, in addition, we know that the voice of God will never contradict the Bible. If I hear a voice telling me something that goes against what the Bible says, it's not from God.

If I ask God for help with making a decision, I ask him to confirm what I've heard through the Bible, other people, and open doors. When those line up, I move forward. When they don't, I wait and keep asking God for clarity.

How will you know when it's God speaking? Jesus says that his sheep recognize his voice (John 10:27–28). You'll know it when you hear it.

Whether you turn to the right or to the left, your ears will hear a voice behind you, saying, "This is the way; walk in it."
ISAIAH 30:21

Prayer: Heavenly Father, thank you that your Word burns in my heart. May I trust you to speak clearly and confirm what I hear.

Blessed are those who "know it when they see it," for they shall recognize the presence of God.

Day 21

"If that is how God clothes the grass of the field, which is here today and tomorrow is thrown into the fire, will he not much more clothe you--you of little faith?"

MATTHEW 6:30

Clothed

CLOTHES ELUDE ME, especially pants. I can try on fifty pair, and not one will fit. A medical issue that caused an unhealthy weight loss has given me a "straight as a stick" shape that doesn't have curves to fit the places curves should go. This leaves baggy fabric where no bag was intended. Discouragement sets in, so I seldom shop.

Touristy beach towns overflow with shops beckoning vacationers, and this one was no exception. Stores displayed shells, sand buckets, shovels, nets, and beach towels. Logo hats and T-shirts fluttered in the breeze on outside racks. While checking out the offerings one day, I found a store with a cute pair of pants displayed in the window. "Right, like those will fit, but I'll try them on anyway. It's vacation, Lord, and you know I need pants."

I thoroughly enjoyed choosing several pair to try on, though completely convinced that I'd put them right back on the rack afterward. On a whim, I even grabbed a cute top to try on with them. The fancy dressing room made trying them on quite festive. As I looked into the mirror, my jaw dropped, and I laughed in disbelief. They fit perfectly. The fabric snuggled comfortably, with no extra bags. I left the store with a big grin, two pair of pants, and the top and fairly skipped to my car.

It took a while for the reality of God's provision to sink in. My two-year search for suitable pants had come to fruition when he handed me not one pair, but two. Friends, there are seasons when God gives us so much that we cannot deny the lavish love he pours out.

I love the word *provision*. A friend of mine uses it frequently, usually gesturing with an open hand while speaking: "God, however you want to answer this prayer is okay with me. I know you are good, and you know the best way to meet this need. You have the solution to the problem." She is confident that God has already prepared whatever is needed.

My friend's trust hasn't come easily or quickly but through a lifetime of circumstances that would have pushed many people to drink or drugs. Those traumas broke her, and she clung to Jesus only.

We became friends shortly before the final "straw." I watched her immerse herself in worship and in books about surrendering hurt and pain to Jesus. Finally, she was able to declare in confidence, "God, I trust your provision in my life, relationally, and financially."

Abraham's journey to faith was also arduous. Twice he called Sarah his sister so that he wouldn't be killed by foreign kings. When it looked as if God had forgotten about his promise to provide an heir from his own body, Abraham listened to Sarah and fathered a child with her maid instead of waiting in faith a bit longer. God worked miracles in the midst of each of Abraham's failures, showing Abraham that he was trustworthy. Sarah finally gave birth to the promised son (Genesis 12, 15, 16, 20, 21).

When God told Abraham to take the son of promise and sacrifice him as a burnt offering, Abraham placed Isaac on the altar and picked up the knife in obedience, only to hear, "Stop, don't harm the boy!" Abraham stopped immediately. He lifted his eyes and saw a ram caught in the thicket. The ram took Isaac's place on the altar, and Abraham called God Jehovah-Jireh (Genesis 22). I discovered that, although Jehovah Jireh translates as "The Lord will provide," its nuanced meaning adds the idea of "will see to it." God perceives our need and personalizes our provision, like the pants he gave me.

When God provided the ram to take Isaac's place, I imagine him witnessing the emotions that must have warred inside Abraham. Even though Hebrews 11:19 tells us that he believed God would raise Isaac from the dead, I wonder if Abraham shed tears of gratitude when the angel pronounced that definitive "Stop!" I wonder how hard he hugged his son as God met needs far beyond the physical with his provision of the ram.

The ram in the thicket represents Jesus, the Lamb, taking the place of our sin on the cross. God the Father figuratively lifted his knife, but no angel stopped him. I wonder if God sorrowfully wept as Jesus died for our sin. I wonder if he then wept for joy when Jesus rose again: when his provision for the biggest need we will ever face—our salvation—was complete.

Friends, we too can trust him and say in faith, "Jehovah-Jireh, you know exactly how to supply anything I require." You can bet he'll even be pretty creative in how he does it.

Financial: Shall we catch a fish, God? (see verse written out below this list)

Emotional: Take me off the rollercoaster and set me on solid ground (Psalm 40:2).

Safety: Shall we build a fort? (Psalm 18:2).

Healing: Worms for medicine, anyone? (see Day 18).

Shelter: You've prepared a place for me (John 14:2).

Anything else: Your priceless wisdom is free for the asking (James 1:5).

> *"So that we may not cause offense, go to the lake and throw out your line. Take the first fish you catch; open its mouth and you will find a four-drachma coin. Take it and give it to them for my tax and yours."*
> MATTHEW 17:27

Prayer: Your Word says you have given us everything we need for life and godliness. Let me open my eyes in wonder as I see your miraculous supply.

Blessed are those who take the risk to try on clothes for the hundredth time, for they will find the provision of God.

Day 22

Do not fear, for I am with you.

ISAIAH 41:10

Cloudy Judgments

CLOUDS DARKENED THE morning sky. *Ugh. It'll be too cold to go out. The wind will whip through my clothes, and I'll freeze.* However, the desire for fresh air, exercise, and the daily treasure hunt won out, so I layered up, determined to go out, if only for a few minutes. First, I put on a base layer and shirt, then a super warm sweater, topped off by a puffer coat. My days living on the Oregon coast have taught me how to face the cold.

I headed out. *Oh, it's not so cold after all. That's surprising.* I shed the puffer coat and tied it around my waist. Soon the sweater ended up tied around my neck. I must have made a pretty ridiculous sight.

God reminded me that I could just have gone out onto the balcony to check what the temperature felt like outside. I didn't. I made a judgment about how comfortable I would be outside based on familiar conditions along the Pacific coast, not the Atlantic. In other words, I didn't fact-check.

On the southern Oregon coast the weather can be miserable. Summers deceptively disguise freezing conditions by allowing the sun to show up in the sky. However, wind strong enough to literally push me around, combined with low temperatures even on sunny days, can make me never want to be outside. Clouds in the summer mean that

I could freeze even with layers of clothing on. It didn't occur to me that the Atlantic coast might be different.

I've made the same kind of mistake in other areas. When frozen yogurt first became a thing, a family member discovered the delicious flavor, but fro-yo wasn't available in the small town where she lived. When she came to visit our small city, she insisted on going to the health food store to get some. I went with her but refused to try it. Gross. I didn't like yogurt, so why would my opinion change just because it was frozen? I refused even the single bite that would have completely changed my mindset. Fast forward thirty years, and now I say, "Let's go."

God showed me that my snap decisions, made without full information, were usually based on fear of the outcome. What if I went outside and became miserably cold? What if I took that bite of frozen yogurt and it tasted terrible? What if I were to reach out to the person who believes differently from me but be unable to answer their questions about Jesus?

Fifteen months before heading to Myrtle Beach, I was trying to figure out ten future life steps at a time. I over-analyzed each step, making myself into a crazy person. Yes, there were times in my days when I trusted God, but just as many when I didn't even look to him but only at the "problem" to be solved.

One agonizing day when I asked God for guidance, he told me to just take one step at a time. He would lead me in each one as the appropriate time came. During the same time period, he brought to mind the old hymn "I Surrender All." Each day when I took my walk in Oregon, I sang the song, sometimes multiple times.

At first when I would sing, fear would well up at the thought of completely surrendering to his will, but I sang the lyrics repeatedly for weeks until I finally meant them. I relinquished my right to know the outcome ten steps ahead of time and handed over the aftermath of my next step to him.

Let me repeat that. I placed my trust where it had belonged all along and surrendered the outcome of my decisions to him. By faith I trusted that he would lead me down the right path. By the time trust finally allowed me to say yes to surrendering, my fear of the future was gone. If little "frighten flutters" threatened to return, I spoke these words out loud: "God, I trust you. You have promised to take care of me. I am yours." I also had several friends praying for me.

I discovered that it's safe to live dangerously with God. What I mean is that I can trust him for the outcome of every situation, even if it feels scary. I can try new adventures without fear. At least this is true when I know he's the One leading me into the situation or decision.

I'd always wanted to go to Myrtle Beach. When I began to research a place to stay for a month's sabbatical, the logistics felt impossible. I thought, *I can't do that. It's too big an undertaking in every way.* Then I came across a rental that had just come back on the market. A couple had been forced to cancel their long-time reservation because of illness, and I was able to rent a small beachfront condo for only $1,000 for a full month. Then my daughter offered to drive with me across the country to get there. With those two gifts in place, God infused me with the courage and excitement to dive into this adventure headfirst. I'm so glad he did.

I witnessed God's power and majesty in the magnificence of the ocean in South Carolina. If I'd had any residual doubt about his ability to guide me and provide for me, it fled in the face of his creation. The ocean creatures, with their unique adaptive features, shouted that he can be trusted. The many gifts he bestowed on me echoed the shout.

Praise God from whom all blessings flow—especially the blessing of courage.

> *"Do not let your hearts be troubled. You believe in God; believe also in me."*
> JOHN 14:1

Prayer: Father, help me to set aside fear and trust you to take me to new places.

Blessed are those who don't make snap judgments, for they shall have the courage to live dangerously, and love dangerously, with God.

Day 23

The sea is his, for he made it.

PSALM 95:5

Rhythms

SITTING ON THE beach, my body relaxed with the sounds of the surf. Steady and rhythmic lapping soothed my mind and increased my awareness of Jesus. I loved how the sound surrounded me whether I was in the condo with the balcony doors open or on the beach.

The rhythms weren't confined to audible content. Watching the waves rush in and then slowly pull out had its own cadence. Mesmerized, my eyes followed them in and out. The movement of the water slowed my breathing and relaxed my muscles. Calm settled in, and peacefulness made me want to remain in this place for hours.

The intensity carried my mind to the power and majesty of Jesus. You might think that, two weeks into this vacation, I'd have become numb to the early lure of the beach and water, but I'm not sure it's possible for me to get tired of the ocean. Just thinking about it now makes me long for the beach experience again.

God created rhythms all around us in life. Our heartbeat and breathing follow a beat. The sun and moon move in a cadence that sets the pattern of days, months, years, and seasons (Genesis 1:14). In fact, God seems to feel that rhythms are important. Even babies bounce and sway to music, smiling and gurgling. They are soothed to sleep with rocking motions. Once they master walking, their legs move to a beat.

Children delight in rhythm, rhyme, and repetition. Their ability to read emerges from having internalized those three. One great part of teaching kindergarten was all the fun words encountered in children's songs and books. One of my favorites, "Six Little Ducks" (public domain) starts with "Down to the river they would go, Wibble wobble wibble wobble ho ho ho." I loved the way the words rolled off my tongue with their meter and rhyme.

We are told that a regular, repeated cadence releases endorphins in our brain, making us happy and content. Just as babies are soothed by a heartbeat, so are adults. A few times in my life when trauma left my body quivering, the shaking stopped only when someone took me in their arms to comfort me. Soon my body responded to their slow breathing and heartbeat, and calmed. There's rhythm in our relationship with God. Since the Bible nowhere explicitly states, "This is the rhythm of your relationship with God," I think it's permissible for us to ponder together what that tempo might look and feel like. I'll bet that each of us might have different ideas or suggest different analogies. Here's one thought (my ponderings, not theological facts): At creation when God breathed the breath of life into Adam, he set in motion the man's heartbeat and breathing. You might say that this was the rhythm of life within Adam. At that point in time no sin estranged Adam from God, so I would assume the breath was both physical and spiritual.

The death and resurrection of Jesus opened the way for each of us to become a new creation. He appeared to the disciples after he arose, breathed on them, and said, "Receive the Holy Spirit" (John 20:22). May I geek out for a minute? The Greek word used in John for "breathed" isn't found anywhere else in the New Testament. It is, however, the same word used by the Septuagint (the first Greek translation of the Old Testament) in Genesis 2:7: "The LORD God formed a man from the dust of the ground and breathed into his nostrils the breath of life, and the man became a living soul." Isn't that cool?

May I take the liberty to suggest that Jesus breathed on them to restore the spiritual rhythm of life in them? Their ability to remain in that flow depended on their listening to, and interacting with, the Holy Spirit. The Holy Spirit enables our heart to beat in time with the heart of Jesus. He leads us, guides us, and speaks deeply within our hearts to either comfort or correct us.

When our physical rhythms get out of whack, our whole body and mind can be affected. My sister's heart went out of sync multiple times in her life. She was rushed to the emergency room with her heart in atrial fibrillation, knowing that, without treatment, the result could be fatal. Afib happens when the top chamber of the heart has an irregular beat. The doctors were able to restore a normal pulse.

It's vital for us to keep rhythms of any kind, but especially faith rhythms, in balance. When you feel your "Jesus heartbeat" getting out of whack, crawl up into his lap and yield yourself to him to let him calm you. Let the Holy Spirit restore the flow of love between you.

When you feel out of sorts because of stress, try a trip to the beach to listen to the waves. That will rebalance pretty much any of us, allowing us a space to sit with Jesus and take in the grandeur. If you can't go in person, find a soundtrack of waves on your computer. Even here in Arizona I can close my eyes, listen to the sounds, and imagine I am at the ocean. I'll save you a seat on the sand, and we can worship Jesus together.

> *The LORD God formed a man from the dust of the ground and breathed into his nostrils the breath of life, and the man became a living being.*
> GENESIS 2:7

Prayer: Lord, keep my walk with you in the rhythm of your grace.

> *Blessed is the person who embraces the soothing rhythms of God, for they shall find the shalom of life.*

Day 24

Who has measured the waters in the hollow of his hand, or with the breadth of his hand marked off the heavens?

ISAIAH 40:12

The Hollow of His Hand

MY GOOD FRIEND has big, capable hands. If I ever comment on them, he says, "You should see my father's hands." Our Father has big hands. As I sit with the warm sand beneath me and stare at the enormous ocean before me, I am reminded that the Bible says God holds the sea in the hollow of his hand (Isaiah 40:12). I can't begin to see all of the ocean at once. How can he possibly hold it all? My hand barely cradles enough for a small sip of tap water.

Vast, immeasurable, expansive, infinite, limitless. If those adjectives evoke an image of the ocean, God's hands must be that much bigger to hold it all. Even if we label those descriptors as hyperbole, we know his hands are big.

Instead of saying, "Uppie, Daddy" (to quote one of my daughters as a toddler) to mean "pick me up in your arms," or "set me on your shoulders," we can say "Uppies," to indicate being scooped up in God's big hands. Think about all the activities we can safely attempt while nested there. We can jump as though we're on a giant trampoline. We can play football with a whole team surrounded in God's palm. We can swim in the ocean. We can cuddle up with a book and read.

I wonder if God might swoosh us around as if we're on an airplane. I'll bet he'd make a good rollercoaster simulation, or maybe he'd cover us up with a blanket and let us sleep.

God's hands protected Moses. When Moses wanted to see more of God, God responded that no one could see his face and live. So, God designed a safe plan: "Then the LORD said, 'There is a place near me where you may stand on a rock. When my glory passes by, I will put you in a cleft in the rock and cover you with my hand until I have passed by. Then I will remove my hand and you will see my back; but my face must not be seen'" (Exodus 33:21–23). What a display of both God's power and his gentleness!

The concept of might and tenderness contained in and even epitomized by the same person fascinates me. It reminds me of old movies where the tough, capable dad faces off with a bad guy to protect his family. He stares down the formidable foe and offers a peaceful solution. When the villain sneers and rushes in to attack, our hero subdues him and then calmly hurries back to comfort his family, soothing them with the touch of his hands.

God's hands protect and comfort me. As I pondered these thoughts, I felt as if God sat down on the sand beside me, took my hand in his, and showed me his glory. In the same way the heavens declare the glory of God (Psalm 19:1), the ocean also declares his splendor. I felt comforted in much the same way I did long ago when my dad held my hand during the thirty-minute midnight walk home on the evening my mom had kicked me out of the house (Day 12).

God's hands are also a safe place for me to wrestle with any life questions I may have, especially questions about faith. I can get out my Bible and snuggle, comfortably ensconced, to reaffirm truth from the original source: God's written Word and the example of Jesus, his incarnate Word. Not anything or anyone else is stronger than God. He is above all. I am completely protected as I figure out life and faith while nestling within the confines of his love and Word.

His wonderful, beautiful hands satisfy us with good gifts, lead us, uphold us, and imbue us with life and breath. They made the sea, the dry land, and everything else in the created cosmos. When we think he has forsaken us, he points out that he has engraved us indelibly onto the palms of those hands. Now, that's love! (See Psalm 139:10, 104:28, and 95:5; Job 12:10; and Isaiah 41:10 and 49:16).

Dear friend, I pray for you as I write, that you will curl up in Abba's hand with a warm blanket and rest. May you set aside the issues that trouble you and breathe peacefully. I ask that you, too, will feel the dichotomy of the mighty power of God coupled with his tender love. They are both so real. "One thing God has spoken, two things I have heard: 'Power belongs to you, God, and with you, Lord, is unfailing love'" (Psalm 62:11–12).

Then maybe we can all go for a walk together on the beach. You can grip one of his hands, and I'll clasp the other. Let's swing them playfully as we go. I think Daddy God will smile, don't you?

> *"I give them eternal life, and they shall never perish; no one will snatch them out of my hand. My Father, who has given them to me, is greater than all; no one can snatch them out of my Father's hand. I and the Father are one."*
> JOHN 10:28–30

Prayer: God, I thank you that you have hands big enough to enfold me during our honest conversations. May I allow you to restore me from any place I have strayed from the truth of your Word. Thank you that no one and nothing can snatch me out of your hand.

Blessed is the person who perceives the vastness of the ocean, for they shall gain understanding of the power of God.

Day 25

"Where your treasure is, there your heart will be also."
MATTHEW 6:21

We're All Looking for Treasure

WE TALK TO others easily, but how comfortably and effectively do we dialogue with God? Encounters with other beachcombers provided the highlights of my day on many occasions as I asked them, "Did you find anything good? What are you searching for today?"

"Oh, yes. I found babies' ears." One searcher eagerly opened her baggie to show me fragile shells that, indeed, looked somewhat like a tiny ear.

Tourists and locals alike enjoyed answering my questions as they lifted up medicine bottles with tiny shark teeth, red buckets filled to the brim with large mollusk shells, and long-handled nets filled with mini shells. One woman I approached replied, "We're all looking for treasure." Her statement struck me as extremely profound. In all of life, all of us are indeed searching for treasure.

The question is, What treasure are we looking for? On the beach people searched for shark teeth and for specific shells, like babies' ears.

They watched for anything unusual washing up onto the shore. They never knew what might be spewed forth from the mysterious depths.

As I've stated before, the real treasure I came to the beach to find was simply uninterrupted time to soak in God's presence and bask in his Word. He went beyond my simple desire and met the deepest need of my heart: to know that I am loved, wanted, forgiven, and delighted in. He reinforced this knowledge daily through dolphins, shells, and whispers to my heart.

I learned to ask God each day what treasure he had for me. The whispers that came in response were just as tangible as the shells I could see with my eyes. God had spent many years helping me cultivate my prayer life before I ever arrived at the beach, and it was my prayer life that opened the door for me to recognize the gifts: the lifeline that allowed me to hear and respond to words like, "Sit down on the sand and look out at the water" (Day 10).

A few days ago, my friend asked me to include some thoughts on prayer in this book. It had never occurred to me that such thoughts would be wanted or needed. She assured me that she herself needed them, so here are some heartfelt thoughts that make my prayer time more intimate.

One big obstacle to prayer is how distant God can feel. Years ago, I knew I needed something to help me feel reassurance that I was talking to a person and not an "it." I began to imagine a picture of God on his throne, based on what I read in Scripture, with Jesus next to him. It helped. Over the years I have imagined other scenarios, like him sitting next to me in church instead of hovering in the air above the pulpit.

One friend shared that she envisions herself on God's lap, as though she is talking to her daddy. Another imagines him sitting in the passenger seat of the car as she drives. You may want to stop for a minute and think of a picture that would help you "see" God.

Many people feel inadequate, concerned that they don't know how to pray. You might want to experiment with a mindset shift, reminding yourself that the way you talk to God can mirror the way you talk to humans. Talk to him the same way you would hang with a friend at the coffee shop. Release a big sigh to clear out the pollution of the day and just start visiting. There is no right or wrong way to chat, other than to avoid babbling on and on about yourself and monopolizing the conversation. Bear in mind that you're talking to the One who loves you more than anyone else could ever do. Have a conversation in which you both talk to God and deliberately quiet your racing thoughts to listen to him.

One difference is that you don't have to talk aloud if you don't want to or can't do so comfortably or unobtrusively when in a public setting. In 1 Samuel 1:13 we read, "Hannah was praying in her heart, and her lips were moving but her voice was not heard." Yet we know that God both heard her silent prayer and answered her.

What about those questions dealing with when to pray, where, and for how long? Well, when, where, and for how long do you talk to your friends? For me, I talk to friends whenever I can, wherever I can, for as long as I can. I have regularly scheduled calls to out-of-town friends and meet in-town friends at impromptu times. I also text friends throughout the day when I want to share a tidbit of information or ask a question. A well-rounded prayer life includes all of these.

Like approaching strangers on the beach, getting started may be the hardest part. Each time we pray, the dialogue becomes more and more natural, until it's automatic. Start with however many minutes you think you have available and ask God to lead you in how to pray. You'll find your prayers gradually becoming less about "Gimme" and more about "How do I walk through this hard situation with grace?" You'll begin to desire his will above your own.

Don't rush this journey. Eventually, you will get to the point at which you have a continual conversation with God that ebbs and flows, winds down and picks back up all day long. This is called praying without ceasing. You'll wonder how you ever made it through your days without talking to him "constantly," even if that means off and on throughout the day as situations arise.

The eyes of the Lord are on the righteous and
his ears are attentive to their prayer.
1 PETER 3:12

Prayer: Lord, we echo your disciples' request, "Teach us how to pray."

Blessed is the person who recognizes treasure beyond their previous
knowledge, for they shall receive above what they ask or imagine.

Day 26

For you who revere my name, the sun of righteousness will rise with healing in its rays.

MALACHI 4:2

Faithful and True

BRISK AIR INVIGORATED me as I walked to the beach in the darkness to await the rising of the sun. Soon brilliant reddish-orange light, with a softer halo of yellow, began to fill the horizon. It reflected off the wet beach in the same way a mirror reflects our image. I'd never before witnessed a sunrise with such vibrant colors. Something about the clouds in the sky seemed to magnify the hues.

Every two minutes the scene changed enough to warrant a new photograph on my phone. The orange and yellow began to swirl together and overtook the entire sky, looking like advancing lava. Gray clouds puffed around, reminding me of smoke.

As the sun climbed higher, the colors muted to pastels, including some pinks, and a smoky gray with hints of lavender. The last pictures I took showed an almost monochromatic gray wash in which the beach blended with the clouds and only a small orb of orange sun peeked through. Unfettered by homes or trees, the view remained spectacular.

I believe that this sunrise was the most incredible I've ever seen, even including others I saw here at the beach. I marveled at the way the spectacle represented the glory of God. Its magnificence constituted my gift for the day.

Later that afternoon I spoke with my daughter on the phone and shared the beauty I'd witnessed. Her comment stopped me in another of those "Duh!" moments. "I don't think I've ever seen a sunrise over the ocean—only a sunset." It was true, I realized, that our sunrises on the West coast had been viewed over land, usually the mountains.

Believe it or not, it hadn't dawned on me that what I was viewing along the Atlantic offered a different perspective from what I had seen all the time in Oregon. I chewed on that thought for days, wondering about its significance, if any. I love the reality that, in any moment of life, an "Aha!" can be found.

Eventually, my thoughts landed on the fact that it didn't matter whether I watched the rising sun over land or sea or even whether I witnessed a sunrise or a sunset. What matters is that the sun never fails us. It has been rising and setting reliably since creation, regardless of the vantage point of the watcher. Adam and Eve observed this exact same sun rise and set over the Garden of Eden. Noah and Abraham saw the same sun also, as did Joseph, Moses, David, and Jesus himself. This reality dawned on me as I regarded that dawn, and it was mind boggling.

A litany of the gifts the sun affords me also flooded my mind. The sun's light allows me to see clearly. Thick, predawn darkness had necessitated my using my phone flashlight to arrive safely on the beach. With no light, I had been able to see only the vaguest of shapes and could easily have tripped. Slowly, as the sun revealed itself, I could begin to discern objects dimly. But only after that orb had fully crested the horizon could I make out crabs and jellyfish—to see them "face to face," so to speak. In much the same way we now get predawn glimpses of God, but one day we will gaze directly and unapologetically into his blessed face (1 Corinthians 13:12).

Basking in the light and warmth produced by the sun just feels good. It's calming, soothing, and causes us to thrive. Scientists have discovered that those feelings are not just subjective. They are real body responses. Without getting academic, let's just say that the sun releases chemicals into our brain and body that bring healing, both mentally and physically.

Let that sink in. The sun has been giving us all these cool benefits since creation, because that is the way the Creator programmed it. The cycle and its benefits never change. Our sun has faithfully been doing its job all these years.

These realizations shout the faithfulness of God. He set into motion this life-giving source that will remain until he creates a new heaven and a new earth. It makes me think about other tangible objects that have endured from creation until now, like the land, sea, plants, animals, and people. Though I don't usually see them as signs of God's enduring love, they are. From now on I want to reframe the daily, the "mundane," in those terms.

Yet God has given us a more important and even more dependable life-giving Source—Jesus, the Son of Righteousness. Basking in his presence brings relaxation and a sense of well-being. He gives us joy, heals the brokenhearted, and binds up our wounds. He comforts those who mourn (John 15:11; Psalm 147:3; and Isaiah 61:1–2). All of those benefits come because, first and foremost, he alone was able to bridge the sin-caused rift in our relationship with God.

God's plan for dealing with sin also shouts his faithfulness. Shortly after creation, when Adam and Eve sinned, God shared his plan for our reconciliation when he told the serpent (Satan) that Eve's offspring would crush his head and that he would strike the heel of her offspring (Genesis 3:15). Thousands of years later, Jesus fulfilled that prophecy.

God the Father, though intangible, is unfailingly faithful. He is the same yesterday, today, and forever (Hebrews 13:8). Just like the sun he set in place and the Son he sent to bridge the gap separating us from God, he never fails us.

> *Because of the Lord's great love we are not*
> *consumed, for his compassions never fail.*
> *They are new every morning; great is your faithfulness.*
> LAMENTATIONS 3:22–23

Prayer: Lord, open my eyes to see the way your faithful love is interwoven into the gifts you gave at creation and the gifts I receive from the sacrifice of Jesus.

> *Blessed are those who recognize that God has never*
> *failed them, for they shall "walk on water."*

Day 27

Give me an undivided heart, that I may fear your name.

PSALM 86:11

Split Focus

I WANTED TO SEE another spectacular sunrise, so the following day I again went to the beach early in the morning. This time, once a little light showed up, I tried to look for new shells and observe the moving sun at the same time. You're pretty smart if you're thinking, *I'll bet that didn't work*. It didn't. Each time I looked back up from seeking shells, I realized that I had missed a nuance of the spectacular display. My split focus caused me to not do well either at collecting shells or at documenting the sunrise.

I often have a split focus in the kitchen. It's too tedious to stand around waiting for something to cook, so I walk away for "just a minute." Meanwhile, I get absorbed in something and forget the stove until I smell something burning. I promise myself that the next time I'll give the pan my full attention, but I don't.

I can't think of any scenario in which a split focus works well. It's especially bad when I divide my attention when I'm around people. When I try to read a text while listening to my grandson, I either don't comprehend the text or don't hear what he says, making him feel overlooked.

Years ago, I attended a Walk Thru the Bible Seminar. The leader talked about David's whole heart toward God, in contrast to Solomon's half-hearted allegiance. Solomon's heart became divided as he chose between God and obedience and again between women and idols.

I pondered what it is that splits our attention from God. Many distractions can pull our thoughts from God. I'll bet you're way ahead of me on what I might name, but some examples that immediately come to mind are my cell phone, friends, music, books, movies, or shopping. While these may all be distracting, we can set boundaries and allow them a place at appropriate times. We're wise to take the time to assess, though, what it is that pulls our heart away from God.

In my life the split focus has been between pleasing God and pleasing people. Early in life I learned to be a people pleaser around my mom so that I wouldn't make her angry. I wanted her to want me in the same way my dad seemed to want me.

Fear of rejection reigned strongly in my heart. I tried, often subconsciously, to control people's opinions of me by saying yes to requests, even if I disliked the activity they were asking me to join. After all, if I said yes they would like me, right?

Being asked to help with events at church made me feel valued, even if the value felt conditional on my functioning as a capable "right hand" person. I didn't feel I had any worth to another person unless I was helping them in some way. I took to the extreme the apostle Paul's injunction to think of others more highly than of myself (Philippians 2:3–5), convincing myself that none of my own needs mattered at all—even my physical needs.

If I over-committed and didn't have the time to keep a promise, I kept it anyway. I would skip meals and burn the candle at both ends for days at a time, pushing my body beyond healthy limits.

No one mastered conflict avoidance better than I did. *Always go along with what the other person says. Just listen, bite your tongue, and say nothing. That way no one will be offended. No one will get mad. Never rock the boat, ensuring that rejection won't happen.*

I would be the first to ask forgiveness if a conflict did arise, even if the other person never acknowledged that they might be wrong. I did that continually, until finally I would explode and in anger point out the other person's offensive attitude or action. If they gave an angry or wounded reaction to my words, I would backtrack immediately, apologizing for what I'd said or for expressing it the wrong way or with a negative attitude.

My fear of rejection and abandonment strangled my trust in God in the area of relationships with others. My actions that appeared to be serving God were actually self-serving to make others think I was a "good Christian."

God used to highlight verses like Galatians 1:10 for me: "Am I now trying to win the approval of human beings, or of God? Or am I trying to please people?" The answer? I was trying to please people. For years as he spoke to me I would repent, but I would fall right back into the destructive habit. This is not to say that my every action was self-serving, but many were.

The turning point enabling me to finally put a stop to people-pleasing over God-pleasing came during tough times a few years ago when I told God I was willing to live in whatever way he wanted me to. Something broke in me that day. He brought me to the old hymn "I Surrender All" as he began to ask me to trust him over all areas of my life, but especially relationships. As previously mentioned, I sang the song daily until my mind and heart were convinced to trust him enough to truly surrender.

When we trust God, walking whole-heartedly before him, we are energized and strengthened. But when we worry about what other people think, we become depleted emotionally, get stressed easily, and have less willpower. God used my time in Myrtle Beach to resolve those very issues. Now I walk confidently in the calling he has set before me and am daily encouraged and strengthened. I pray that he will do the same for you.

Whether it be people pleasing or some other issue, choose to bring your focus, your heart, and your trust to God and God alone.

"They loved human praise more than praise from God."
JOHN 12:43

Prayer: O God, give me an undivided heart. Let me care more about what you think than about what other people think.

Blessed are those who don't split their focus, for they shall be whole-hearted for God.

Day 28

Let us walk in the light of the Lord.

ISAIAH 2:5

Perspective

I WALKED SLOWLY DOWN the beach once again, breathing in the wonders of the day. I took my time, alternating between staring at the water while I stood in the shallow surf and moving on down the beach. My handy bucket hung from my hand, ever ready to hold my "catch of the day."

Even after having spent three weeks doing the same search every day, it had never grown old because it was never really the same. Each time a wave rushed over the sand, that wave held the potential to leave behind a new and different treasure. The wonder and mystery made the hunt unique every morning.

I gathered shells as I walked toward the sun, which was reflecting off the water and sand. By the time I turned around to go back, the bucket held great bounty. I leisurely returned the way I had come with my back now to the sun, shielding a bit of the glare. I gained a totally new perspective. The differing light accentuated beautiful shells I might otherwise have missed.

This reminded me of a time when I had visited my daughter. While she was at work, I had decided to clean her apartment oven since her wrist issues prevented her from scrubbing off the ground-in grime. The small kitchen had only one overhead light, making it difficult for me to see where greasy dirt still lurked. After doing the best I could on one side, I moved around the oven door to the second side. To my surprise, light filled the oven. My body had been blocking the sunshine from the window. The second side took only half as long because I could see so well.

Light makes all the difference in our perspective. It's pretty obvious in our earthly life how good lighting keeps us from tripping or falling or from getting bruised by running into a hazard. Good light allows us to clearly see the dirt on our hands, kitchen floor, or car. I can gain illumination inside my house by turning on a light or opening the curtains during the day.

What about our spiritual light?

I love the book of John, where we are told in chapter 1, verses 4–5, "In him was life, and that life was the light of all mankind. The light shines in the darkness, and the darkness has not overcome it." People walking in spiritual darkness could see Jesus but not perceive who he really was. Their perspective was skewed by what they were letting into their hearts.

Our perspective on hurt, pain, illness, rejection, or betrayal depends on the amount of light or darkness we allow to permeate the situation. Darkness says, "Retaliate. Hurt them the way they hurt you. Don't accept their apology, even if they acknowledge the devastation their actions have caused and ask forgiveness. They deserve to hurt the way you hurt." When we listen to darkness, unforgiveness and bitterness take root, and those attitudes block out the light. As much as we want to say that unforgiveness is okay, that our perpetrator is deserving of the bitterness festering in our heart, it's not okay. Infections that fester inside harm *us*, and bitterness is an infection of the soul. Unforgiveness is an infection of the spirit.

Ephesians 4:32 enjoins us, "Be kind and compassionate to one other, forgiving each other, just as in Christ God forgave you." We may not want to forgive, and taking this stance may be indescribably difficult, but if you allow the light of Christ into your heart and mind, it will happen. It must happen. God tells us to forgive.

When I think of all that Christ has forgiven me, the recognition softens my mindset, and I realize that I need to extend the same to others. (Remember that we talked about forgiveness on Day 17.) I'll leave it to you to ponder on your own the sterner command found in Matthew 6:14–15.

Light implores the opposite. Jesus invites, "Let me hold you while you cry. I know what betrayal feels like. I understand a broken heart. Let me hold your hand in the midst of this pain and silence the voice of the enemy as he questions the reality of your value. You matter—infinitely so!

"Allow unforgiveness to be washed away with the healing salve of my blood and your tears. When the mingled blood and tears have accomplished their work, you will find in yourself a heart that stands ready to pray for the one who has hurt you, be that person friend or foe. Those prayers free me to work both in their life and in yours. Light walks with you through the darkest of storms."

Jesus declared, "I am the light of the world. Whoever follows me will never walk in darkness, but will have the light of life" (John 8:12). If I am following Jesus, I won't pursue where darkness tries to lead me, for that path would lead only to death in my soul. I will follow instead the words of light: the actions and thoughts that bring life.

The strength of God within us declares that we are capable of letting the Light of the World change our perspective in even the toughest circumstance. "In this world you will have trouble. But take heart! I have overcome the world," Jesus reminds us in John 16:33. You can do it. I can do it. His light and life open the way.

> *The city does not need the sun or the moon to shine*
> *on it, for the glory of God gives it light, and the Lamb*
> *is its lamp. The nations will walk by its light.*
> REVELATION 21:23–24

Prayer: Lord, may I let your light shine into my heart even when darkness surrounds me. May I remember that light always wins over darkness.

Blessed is the one who lets light change their
perspective, for they shall be given life.

Day 29

The prudent see danger and take refuge.

PROVERBS 22:3

Dangers of the Deep

ALONG THE PACIFIC Ocean the ruggedness of the Oregon coast contributes to its striking beauty. Narrow, winding highways sit atop the high cliffs, allowing the viewer to see across the water till it blends into the horizon. This beauty contrasts with the perils of those cliffs. Cars that careen over the edge crash to certain tragedy. Slippery rocks create risk to hikers climbing up from the bottom.

In a similar way the beach itself holds dangers. A beachcomber stranded by a high tide faces the real possibility of being crushed against the rocks by thunderous waves. Undertows can strike unexpectedly, dragging people under the water. Anyone living in a coastal town knows the potential for problems and remains vigilant, both for themselves and for others when near the water or cliffs.

The Atlantic coast, in contrast, appears tranquil and serene. The gently undulating sand seems tame in comparison to the Pacific shoreline. In fact, I remember in a teacher education class our professor laying down on the floor a relief map of the United States and inviting discussion as to which coast provided easier land access to early explorers. The dramatic difference between the two coastlines fascinated me, with the Atlantic a clear winner for inviting exploration.

I sat on the beach one day and remembered that long-ago lesson. I pondered dangers, both obvious and subtle, and realized that the Atlantic Ocean poses dangers of its own. They are just more subtle because the ocean looks so calm that it's tempting to let down our guard and fail to recognize perilous situations in time. We might venture into the water beyond our ability to swim back or be unaware of other hidden dangers, like poisonous marine life.

Spiritual danger, too, lurks no matter where we live. "Your enemy the devil prowls around like a roaring lion looking for someone to devour" (1 Peter 5:8). *Prowl. Roar. Devour.* Satan wants to swallow us up and destroy us. He knows no boundaries in seeking that end and employs both obvious and subtle tactics.

We've likely all heard those voices in our mind that declare that we are not good enough, not smart enough, not pretty enough, not worth enough. The voices are intrusive and feel so real that they are difficult to ignore. When they sound so insistent and truthful, it's easy to agree with them, to engage in self-talk such as, *I might as well give up. I'm such a loser. Why am I trying to pretend that I can live for Jesus?* We may even think we've already sinned so much that Jesus won't want us. I hope you've read enough in this book to know that this is a lie. Our Lord always wants us to be with him. Restoring relationships is the reason he came to earth.

Peter enjoins us not to let our enemy push us around but, instead, to resist him (1 Peter 5:9). Sometimes it's easy for us to counter him with, "Go away, enemy. That's not true. I am loved by Jesus and have been bought by his death on the cross." But at other times the voices are so loud and oppressive that we feel too weak to resist them. In those times we must swallow any pride and ask a friend or two to pray for us.

The purpose of the boisterous, demeaning voices is to lead us away from Jesus. The enemy wants to discourage us enough that we will step into sin. He doesn't care so much what kind of sin; any lapse he thinks he can convince us to slip into works for him. He wants us to get so mired in that it feels impossible for us to escape. But what we need to keep in mind is that this is precisely the point at which Jesus reaches out for us.

Years ago, Misty Edwards sang a powerful song that ponders what love looks like. She declares that love showed itself at the cross. Jesus's heart was exposed when his arms were nailed, wide open, on the cross.

Dangers of the Deep

The song "Arms Wide Open" beautifully portrays Jesus looking at us with penetrating eyes as he hangs there dying on our behalf.

It's those protective arms of Jesus, held open in an invitation to embrace us, that break sin's hold on our lives. When we truly see the full picture of the cross and begin to grasp its implications, we weep before him, realizing that our sin is what bloodied his body. Our sorrowful, repentant heart seeks his forgiveness.

Jesus's blood dissolves the wall that was built up when we fell and frees us from that point on from the grip of sin. Friend, we don't have to loll in the muck and mire of anything our enemy has trapped us into doing. Our Savior and Lord still loves us—eternally and infinitely so. Really. Just ask him to forgive you.

When someone around us sins, I hope we open our arms and welcome them into our heart in the same way Jesus offers to welcome them. We weep *for* them until they, too, are caught up in the evocative gaze of Jesus's love. We love and pray until they are able to weep for themselves at the foot of the cross and receive the gift of his cleansing blood. We then weep *with* them, both with joy and with sorrow over any consequences of their sin they may still face. We walk with them through those consequences with a tough love that supports them, while refusing to enable them to continue along the path of destruction.

Then we rejoice together for the miracle of a life saved from danger and transformed.

> "A new command I give you: Love one another. As I
> have loved you, so you must love one another."
> JOHN 13:34

Prayer: Jesus, when I succumb to temptations my enemy lobs at me, may I confess my sin and believe that you forgive me. When my brother or sister is entrapped in sin, let me not be afraid of "contamination." Instead, may I weep with them and open wide my arms to welcome them back into the fold.

Blessed is the one who is alert to potential danger even in scenes of beauty, for they shall be saved from the snares of their enemy.

Day 30

You created my inmost being; you knit me together in my mother's womb.
PSALM 139:13

Colorful Characters

> Mary, Mary, quite contrary
> How does your garden grow?
> With silver bells and cockle shells,
> And pretty maids all in a row.

THIS NURSERY RHYME from my youth intersected with my days at Myrtle Beach. Who knew that "cockle shells" referred to real shells? I thought they were just fun words to mouth.

Nope. It turns out that the most abundant shells on the beach—my beautiful, ruffled-edged-plethora-of-colors-treasures—were in fact cockle shells. My balcony was filled with rows of them in multiple colors and every size imaginable.

I wondered how there could be so many different colors. What caused the variation? I googled the question and found out that some shells take color pigment from what they eat, while others manufacture their own pigment that matches their background to create protective camouflage. Some shells take on colors that shout to potential predators, "I'm poisonous. Hahaha. You'll regret eating me." The image of a shell strutting around taunting its foe cracks me up. It reminds me of a child running and chanting in a sing-song voice, "You can't catch me."

Then come the shy, inhibited shells that hide in their camo, hoping that no one will notice them. The leader admonishes the noisier ones, "Shhh, the fish will hear you. Be quiet." As they swim around looking for their own food, they keep looking over their shoulders for predators. They freeze when they see one.

The image of these two different types of characters, while funny, points out that the purpose of the color embedded in their shell appears in every case to be protection. The vulnerable creatures within their "armor" are protected either by advertising their poisonous nature or by minimizing themselves to stay out of danger's sight.

We people, like these shells, have colorful characters embedded within us, regardless of our age, size, or shape. Positive character traits, such as honesty, perseverance, respect, friendship, responsibility, and kindness are considered important enough that we actively teach them in elementary school. Charts, curriculums, skits, and songs help instill constructive character attributes into our young.

Why do we work so hard to implant character and integrity? May I suggest that good, productive character protects us. First of all, when we possess it we recognize negative character. For example, in the same way shells of certain colors warn other animals to stay away, traits like dishonesty and disrespect can warn the alert, "I'm poisonous. Don't get too close!" At its extreme, such negative traits can fuel abuse. At the least they can jade our spirits and rob us of our sense of value.

The behavior of predators changes in response to the poisonous, shell-bearing animals. They either steer clear or get sick. They may even die. Consequences for us when we ignore the warning signs others may emit are similar. When we don't steer clear of those with negative character traits, our soul can get "sick" or even begin to die.

Observing life shows us that good character helps prevent us from falling into evil, like the corruption unregulated power can bring. Good character leads to greater well-being, and makes us feel good. Researchers have objectively proven these statements to be true.

God was way ahead of us on this issue. He knew the protection good character provides, instilling it into our psyches from creation. Paul enjoins us in Philippians 4:8 to *think about* whatever is true, noble, right, pure, lovely, admirable, excellent, and praiseworthy.

Paul also told the Philippians to put into practice whatever they had received, heard, or seen in him, promising the peace of God would then be with them. There, right there. See it? Paul says that good character will bring the peace of God. God knew when he created us that, if we would only put into practice godly, wholesome thoughts and actions, we would find peace.

Even on a tranquil beach we cannot experience full peace if there is a dissonance between our beliefs and our actions. In fact, if our words and actions don't match, eventually the discord will cause us to change either one or the other. We will either alter our behavior or recalibrate our character. The direction of our choice—whether positive or negative—is greatly influenced by the degree to which we hang out with God and with godly friends.

One year I taught a small group of struggling fifth-grade math students. We studied character traits along with math, because they needed the instruction. When reviewing for an end-of-term exam, I asked the class what concepts we had been learning. One girl raised her hand and said, "We have been learning how to be characters." Aside from laughing inside, recalling her words gives me pause to ask God whether my actions show that I am a character or that I have good character. Since character can change over time, maybe there's still hope for our friend, Contrary Mary.

Who knew that nursery rhymes and colorful shells could teach us so much? Let's think on things that are good, noble, and true and align our actions with our thoughts.

> *Good character is the best insurance; crooks
> get trapped in their sinful lust.*
> PROVERBS 11:6 (MSG)

Prayer: God, impact me to recognize how critical it is that my actions match my words. May peace come to myself and, through me, to those around me.

*Blessed are those who ponder colorful characters, for they
shall glimpse the protection godly character brings.*

Day 31

No one can lay any foundation other than the one already laid, which is Jesus Christ.

1 CORINTHIANS 3:11

Foundations

WALKING BAREFOOT IN the sand delighted me each day. In addition to all the cool treasures I found, interesting people I met, and amazing beauty, the exercise strengthened my legs and feet. When I first arrived in Myrtle Beach, some muscle strain and weakness hampered my ability to walk very far. Each day I added more distance, gauging it by the rainwater ducts spaced along the beach and being careful not to overdo. By the time I left, I could hike a couple of miles down the shore.

As I gained strength to explore more of the beach, God reminded me of years ago when I had been seeing a physical therapist to relieve pain in my shoulder. After a thorough check of range of motion and muscle function, her conclusion surprised me: "After your initial injury, the exercises you have worked on built up the outer layer of muscles without strengthening the deeper, foundational ones. We need to back up and address the inner layers. That's what's causing the pain. They can't handle the same amount of weight the outer ones can."

Frustration often mounted as I began what felt like baby exercises compared to what I had been doing. I wanted to graduate from isometrics against the wall and arm lifts. With the therapist's encouragement,

I continued until, at last, her assessment proved to be correct, and the muscle strength became balanced.

Spiritually, we can get off balance and forget that Jesus is our foundation. "No one can lay any other foundation than the one already laid, which is Jesus Christ. If anyone builds on this foundation using gold, silver, costly stones, wood, hay or straw, . . . fire will test the quality of each person's work"(1 Corinthians 3:11–13).

We are to build our lives on him. When we don't, it's easy for us to fall away from our faith, as in the parable Jesus told about the wise man and the foolish man. One built his house on the rock, and, when the storms came, the structure stood solid. The other built his house upon the sand, and, when the storms came, it fell "with a great crash" (Matthew 7:24–27).

It's easy to inadvertently begin to erect our spiritual "house" on shifting, drifting sand. We can start to trust in our own skills and abilities as our foundation. Years ago, the pastor of the church I attended repeatedly asked a friend of mine to teach Bible studies. The pastor knew that the person held a professional job and came to church every Sunday. Beyond that, the two had never spent time getting to know each other personally. The pastor didn't realize that my friend did not spend any time with the Lord other than on Sundays: no Bible reading, no prayer, no worship. My friend prepared for the Bible study by going over the questions in the teacher's guide an hour before the class started, and the person's leadership and conversational skills allowed them to do an ostensibly good job.

My friend, however, lacked the foundation of knowing the love of Christ intimately, having spent no time building a relationship with him. Eventually, the footing did crash. As happens so often when people work together, a conflict arose. Without a strong friendship with Jesus, my friend didn't know how to deal with the perceived offense against them. The upshot was that this indvidual left the church, never to return. In fact, they never returned to any church.

This outcome could have been prevented by recognition in both the pastor and my friend that the foundational muscle of leaning on Jesus was weak. I pray that, if you are a leader recruiting people for positions at church, you will know each person well before attempting to fit them into place. I also pray that, if you are the one who doesn't yet have strong muscles, you will respond with "Not yet" when asked to serve in some capacity. Work on getting your substructure solid, . . . and then say yes.

It's also tempting for us to begin to trust another person more than Jesus. Many pastors and leaders speak great wisdom as they teach us God's Word. We hungrily eat up all they say and even begin to quote them to other people. All of that is well and good . . . unless we cross over into idolizing them, into placing them on a pedestal.

Emotional maturity is tied to spiritual maturity. I wish I had realized earlier how the automatic reactions programmed into me from childhood and my early adult years had affected the growth of my spiritual muscles. Although those atrophying muscles did grow, they weren't as strong as they could have been, and they definitely weren't balanced. Over time, especially during the last several years, God has dealt with those reactions. I have shared many of them in this book. Mostly they had to do with relational trust. I had to put my "trust focus" on Jesus, not on people.

Remember that our foundation is Jesus. The muscles we use to build on that bedrock are faith and trust. I need to check myself frequently to see if I am utilizing those foundational muscles or if I have started to depend on the outer muscles of my own skills and abilities . . . or on other people.

> *"Everyone who hears these words of mine and puts them into practice is like a wise man who built his house on the rock. The rain came down, the streams rose, and the winds blew and beat against that house; yet it did not fall, because it had its foundations on the rock."*
> MATTHEW 7:24–25

Prayer: Lord, show me where my footing is weak. Show me how to strengthen foundational issues so I can stand firm and victorious during life's difficulties.

Blessed is the one who has their foundation in Jesus, for they shall stand strong.

Day 32

Godliness with contentment is great gain. For we brought nothing into the world, and we can take nothing out of it.

1 TIMOTHY 6:6–7

Simplicity

STANDING STILL AS a statue in the ankle-deep water, my grandson stared off into the distance. Suddenly, he exclaimed, "Whoa!" and ran straight back to the dry sand as a large wave followed him. Over and over again, he ran out, stood, and raced back.

We eventually transitioned to wandering around in search of shells. Consistently, he picked up shell fragments rather than waiting to find complete shells. I prodded him, "There are some whole shells over there. Would you like to look there?"

"No, Grandma. I like these."

The colors and textures drew my grandson more than did the size of the piece he discovered. In looking back, this makes sense. His artistic eye views the world in lines, shapes, and colors. He describes cartoon scenes in terms of the lines placed to indicate action. His world is simple.

Later that day my daughter and I asked my grandson if he preferred to go on a dolphin cruise or a helicopter ride. Adventure opportunities abound in Myrtle Beach, but he declined all suggestions until I mentioned a small playground located in an outdoor shopping area.

"Yes. Yes. I want to go to the playground."

Upon arriving at the shopping area, we stopped first at a restaurant to fill up our energy tanks. Next, we browsed some fun, touristy shops; sat in giant wooden Adirondack chairs that would have been too big for Goliath; and finally followed the wooden boardwalk to a children's haven—a place of respite from the boredom of adult shopping.

A black wrought-iron fence kept the children safe from wandering out into the nearby roadway or to the waterway on the opposite side. Weary parents collapsed into chairs lining the fence, while children twirled from overhead circular monkey bars. A huge, two-part play structure filled the middle of the play area. Access to the peak required either walking up some easy steps or climbing up a log leaning against the toy. After they had reached a landing area, multiple choices beckoned. Children could burrow into a small treehouse, cross the swinging rope bridge to the other section, or circle down the twisty slide.

"Grandma, climb up with me. It's super easy. You can do it." We played for a couple of hours. Up and down. Over and across. He ran up, and I huffed up. I tag teamed with my daughter so neither of us would be completely worn out. We laughed at my grandson's antics. On the way back to the car, we had worked up enough of an appetite to grab a pizza for dinner.

Did you notice that our full day included only simple activities? Interacting with each other face-to-face brought the most pleasure of all. Imagination reigned as we ran on the beach in the morning and played on toys in the afternoon, ignoring the glitter of attractions like Ripley's Believe It or Not.

Nature lends itself to seeing life in a less complicated way. Most of my life I have complicated matters more than necessary. Whether chores, grocery lists, friendships, or even trauma, I tend to get stuck on unnecessary details. I over-analyze and under-trust.

A couple of weeks ago I met a family member for a doctor's appointment. My daughter was to meet us there as well. As the time drew close, I noticed on my Find My Friend app that my daughter had turned into the wrong entrance. Not trusting that she would quickly find the correct building, I called her. I ended up confusing matters and causing her to take more time.

I've done that kind of thing a lot in life, often with much bigger matters. Yet God directs us not to lean on our own understanding but to trust him, promising that he will direct us (Proverbs 3:5–6). It certainly seems that most of our life decisions, big and small, come back to trust.

In the year prior to my heading to Myrtle Beach, God instructed me to take one step at a time. Looking too far ahead and trying to figure out the future would only result in stress. Just one trustful step at a time was needed, especially if that one was all I could at the time clearly visualize.

That one change in my modus operandi simplified my life. Pray. Step. Trust. Notice and accept God's guidance and answers. Pray, step, trust again. Be alert to God's guidance and answers. Step by step, he walked me through a very difficult relational issue and brought me to a place of blessing I had doubted I could ever reach.

You may be in a complicated situation, perhaps even one that is unsafe. I believe he can walk you through it step by step. You may laugh and counter, "Yeah, that's easy for you to say. You don't know my circumstances. It doesn't work that way for all of us."

May I ask you to look again? You may be in the most impossible seeming state of affairs known to humankind, but it's in those very cases that God can work miracles. Daniel faced an untenable situation, but he made a choice to keep praying to God even after a decree from King Nebuchadnezzar threatened his life if he did so. The king threw Daniel in a lions' den, but God sent angels to close the mouths of the lions (Daniel 6:5–23). God is still able to shut the mouths of lions.

Jesus Christ is the same yesterday, today, and forever.
HEBREWS 13:8

God, let me trust that, since you remain the same throughout eternity, you can do the same for me that you did for Daniel. Help me not to worry about the future but to take one step at a time and trust you to guide me.

Blessed is the person who values simplicity,
for they shall see God move.

Day 33

"Do not come any closer," God said. *"Take off your sandals, for the place where you are standing is holy ground."* Then he said, *"I am the God of your father, the God of Abraham, the God of Isaac and the God of Jacob."*

EXODUS 3:5–6

The Shoe

I FOUND A SHOE on the beach. Not a lost shoe left behind by a human, but a shoe dropped by God.

"Riiiiiiight?" you say. "But shoes are made by people, not by God."

Not this shoe. God fashioned a shell to look just like a fairy-sized running shoe and dropped it on the beach. A sense of awe washed over me as I came to realize that God had once again provided a beautifully tailored gift.

The shoe carried deep meaning for me, as my family has been involved in the running shoe industry for years. At one point both my daughter and my son-in-law worked at Nike, and my son-in-law still does. Prior to Nike, my daughter worked at Adidas for several years. So, when I saw the shoe I thought of them.

My thoughts also drifted to my other daughter, a dedicated runner. I recalled her jogging with her son here on the beach last week, making me smile. The several half-marathons she ran in her adult life brought to life her favorite preschool phrase, "Race guys."

Only God knew that the shell shoe represented more to me than just another fun beach find—it represented family. In humility I bowed before the God of the universe with a grateful heart. Why would the King of kings and Lord of lords care enough to bless me so abundantly; to build me up every day? I guess for the same reason he died on the cross for me, for you, for all of us: his love.

Images of God's majesty swirled in my mind as I thought of Moses encountering him at the burning bush. "Take off your sandals, for the place where you are standing on holy ground," God instructed (Exodus 3:5). In reverence and fear Moses, humbler than anyone else on the face of the earth, obeyed (Numbers 12:3). In that place made holy by God's presence, the Lord commissioned Moses to lead the children of Israel out of Egypt, with precise directions on how to approach both Pharoah and the Hebrew elders.

Joshua similarly stood on holy ground to receive his commission to lead the children of Israel into the promised land. When near Jericho, possibly scouting out the city, Joshua looked up and saw a man standing in front of him. Upon hearing the "man" describe himself as the commander of the Lord's army, Joshua fell facedown in reverence and heard the same words Moses had heard: "Take off your sandals, for the place where you are standing is holy" (Joshua 5:15). There the commander gave him battle plans for Jericho.

Moses and Joshua humbled themselves by taking off their sandals. It's spiritually healthy for us to remove our shoes. What does that look like today? In a literal and simple sense, it can mean exactly that. In a symbolic show of humility, we actually take off our shoes and bow our heads. Humility is still valued in God's eyes. As we lay down our pride, we become open to learning from God and others. We have courage to admit when we don't know something. We gain peace from not having to keep up a false front that proclaims we can handle everything on our own.

Demonstrating reverence and awe within our hearts is another way to "take off our shoes." In deference we recognize God's power, might, and worth. We acknowledge the honor he deserves. Bowing before him negates any arrogance of trying to stand before God thinking we have anything to offer him other than our love.

Taking off our shoes physically leaves us vulnerable. In the event of danger, our speed will be seriously compromised, so much so that we may not be able to get away. Spiritually, being barefoot can also render us feeling unprotected. In order to willingly walk without shoes, we must believe that God is safe.

Is God safe? The fire within the bush Moses saw makes me think of the tongues of fire on the disciples' heads when the Holy Spirit was given at Pentecost (Acts 2:3–4). The bush on the mountain held the fire of God, and yet it didn't consume the bush. The same is true of the Holy Spirit in us. "Do you not know that your bodies are temples of the Holy Spirit, who is in you, whom you have received from God?" asks Paul rhetorically (1 Corinthians 6:19–20). We hold the fire of God's Spirit without being consumed, even though when he speaks our hearts may feel as if they are burning within us (Luke 24:32).

God told Moses not to come any closer to him, so Moses heard God's message from a distance. We no longer need to listen from far away, since the Holy Spirit dwells within us. The presence of God doesn't get any closer than that: we hear his voice from the inside!

I walked barefoot on the beach most days, including the day I found the tiny shoe shell. I relished the freedom as my feet gained sensory input that rejuvenated them. Taking off my shoes before God renews my spirit, just as humility frees me to experience him in greater fullness.

Humble yourselves before the Lord, and he will lift you up.
JAMES 4:10

Prayer: Almighty God, may I always remember to come before you in reverence and awe, giving you the honor that your name deserves.

"Blessed are the meek [humble] for they will inherit the earth." Matthew 5:5

Day 34

Worship the Lord in the splendor of his holiness.
1 CHRONICLES 16:29

I Can Only Imagine

WATCHING THE GENTLE waves lap rhythmically at the shore and feeling the light breeze carrying the salty scent of the ocean soothed my soul. The brilliant canvas of swirled blues and whites in the sky, while the horizon stretched endlessly, invited contemplation. Seagulls glided gracefully overhead. Each step along the water's edge brought a sense of calm and connection to the beauty, resulting in my natural response of worshiping God. Worship music playing from my phone wove into the experience.

Several mornings while listening, I heard the song "I Can Only Imagine" playing. The scenic beauty accentuated the power of the lyrics and the melody. My mind became caught up in the reality of heaven, and I wondered if I would either stand in awe when I saw Jesus or kneel at his feet. Would I speak his praises or fall silent? As I raised my arms and worshiped my God in the middle of a magical wonderland of sand and sea, I wept in awe.

Images from the movie by that title invaded my thoughts. The storyline transparently opens up the depths of tragedy and victory played out in the life of songwriter Bart Millard, singer for the band Mercy Me. Abused by his father until he left home, Bart never seemed to be able to find the singing success he sought.

Then, as only God can do, he used a terminal illness to bring Bart's father to redemption through Jesus, causing him to seek Bart's forgiveness, which Bart was finally able to give. The song "I Can Only Imagine," which catapulted Mercy Me into mainstream attention, was born out of Bart's processing his grief over his father's death.

Life, death, grief, and hope all flooded through me. Tears came as I remembered my own mom's struggle with alcoholism and her subsequent death at the age of fifty-five. I processed through the transformation God had wrought in her life. I also remembered the death of my sister at age sixty-two and her telling us all to "meet her under the lemon tree" when our turn came to join her in heaven.

Not only did my surroundings make it easier for me to imagine heaven, but so did my having been born after the resurrection of Jesus. As New Testament followers of Jesus, think of the advantages we have over Old Testament believers just by having the New Testament available to us.

The four Gospels give us firsthand testimony of Jesus himself. His words and actions are recorded in these primary sources, inviting us to understand who he is. The "I Am" came down to show us unambiguously who it is we will walk with in heaven. Though the book of Revelation gives us glimpses of *what* heaven may look and sound like (more on that in Day 36), it's the *who* we'll encounter there that matters so much more. God the Father, Jesus the Son, and the Holy Spirit together set the atmosphere of heaven, just as one person in particular, often the mom, establishes the atmosphere of our homes.

We know that the atmosphere of heaven radiates with life-giving wholeness, because on earth Jesus modeled for us life-giving words and actions. He treated people with dignity, responded to conflict with truth, and provided for people with compassion. Jesus himself declared that, if we have seen him, we have seen the Father (John 14:9). The children of Israel saw God from a distance as he provided for them in the wilderness. We get to see him up close through Jesus.

The lyrics to "I Can Only Imagine" lead us through heart-searching questions about our reactions when we do in fact one day see Jesus in his glory. Those questions ponder our heavenly response, but what about how we react to him now? How do we, now in this earthly phase of eternity, enter into his presence and live there?

Bart Millard had a breakthrough in the music industry only when he quit striving and wrote from his heart—out of his stance of forgiveness.

Only then, as he pondered what his dad was seeing, and what he himself would see in heaven, did Bart touch hearts and lives with his singing. He ceased to care about success and sang instead from his heart. As we bare our hearts, we touch lives also.

Each one of us has a "song" within us that God wants to pour out upon the world: a mountain stream of lyrics, an ocean wave of poetry, a sunset-over-the-ocean painting. A gift of mercy that listens to the heartache of another and, through our extending empathy, understanding, and love, sings life into that person as they at last feel seen, heard, and validated.

Helping clean house for an invalid unable to handle the chore paints a picture of the compassion of God. Just as art stirs our heart with both joy and longing, so does the gift of a helping hand. We need only look at the gift to receive joy. Its beauty evokes a longing for more joy.

Extending friendship to someone who feels unlovable creates deep bonds between two people. A rhythm of love and grace knits their two hearts in a poetic way, and the living poem touches emotions beyond them as others watch and listen.

Endeavors such as song writing, poetry, and painting mirror the creativity of God as he ignites our imaginations. His inspiration moves us as we offer gifts of mercy, help, and friendship. When we approach God with a pure heart, desiring to express our love for him with our talents, skills, and gifts, God's creativity knows no limit.

Now to him who is able to do immeasurably more than all we ask or imagine, according to his power that is at work within us . . .
EPHESIANS 3:20

Prayer: Creator God, I surrender my imagination to you. Bring forth wholesome thoughts to fuel my words and actions. May I hear and repeat the song you have given me to bless the world around me.

Blessed is the one who imagines what it will be like to see Jesus, for they shall be given an expectant heart.

Day 35

I will be satisfied as with the richest of foods; with singing lips my mouth will praise you.

PSALM 63:5

You've Got This— You Trained for It

"YOU'VE GOT THIS! You trained for it! Oh! Oh! Come on, you've got this!" With every muscle tense, my grandson's eyes were glued to our Medieval Times Tournament knight as he screamed encouragement. The field spotlights accentuated the sparks flying as swords from the two knights clashed in this Myrtle Beach tourist attraction. Suddenly, the tension heightened when our knight's shield broke, leaving him vulnerable. We held our breath as his attending page raced out with a new one. Would he make it in time?

Our knight had prevailed in the jousting competitions, with his horse thundering full speed down the sandy indoor arena toward his opponent. He had also won the hand-to-hand combat battles. Now, in this final championship match, he fought with all his might to gain the privilege of protecting the throne.

Throughout the evening our knight's training became evident. Anticipating the moves of his opponent, he skillfully manipulated a myriad of weapons. Multiple battles demanded great endurance. Even when his page replaced broken shields or weapons, his movements had the graceful precision wrought from practice.

Any competitive endeavor starts with drills. If you've ever been on a sports team, you know what I mean. My fifth-grade basketball team practiced dribbling, bounce passes, and chest passes. We ran laps to build endurance. After we had mastered these basic skills, we put them all together in a scrimmage to experience what might happen in an actual game. Then we were ready to meet up with an opposing team.

My daughter joined a soccer team in the first grade. She enjoyed all the drills, kicking with enthusiasm. However, the first game came after only two practices, and no practice game. She and her teammates were shocked when their opponents fought to take the ball away. She got overwhelmed and injured, having mistaken the practice for the real goal—to successfully perform in the actual game.

Our evening at the Medieval Times Tournament ended with our knight losing his last battle, but my grandson's words stuck with me. I wondered, "Have I trained well, Lord? Have I truly absorbed your lessons?" I also wondered whether I at times mistake drills for real engagement.

Our goal in spiritual training is to gain intimacy with God the Father and God the Son through the inner workings of the Holy Spirit. That intimacy results in trust and peace and also allows us to recognize our enemy, whose goal is to keep us away from God. But how do we get there? We engage in the drills.

We read the Bible and study. While this is not the end goal, the Word is our source of truth about who God is and what he's like. It's our anchor to discern truth from lies. Our enemy is a master liar who loves to lead us astray with whispered falsehoods, like "God could never love someone who sinned the way you did." The Bible allows us to enter vicariously into the lives of other sinners like ourselves, revealing the truth of how much God loved people like David, who had committed murder and adultery, and Samson, who leaned on his own strength most of his life, instead of on God.

Studying the Bible isn't about gaining more head knowledge but about learning to recognize God in the midst of life. We absorb his nature to the point that we assimilate and internalize the way he dealt with nations and individuals. Because the Bible is the living Word, it helps me delve deeper and get closer to God.

What do I mean by living Word? I mean as we are reading or studying, the Holy Spirit highlights truths and brings them alive in our hearts. "Were not our hearts burning within us while he talked with us on the road and opened the Scriptures to us?" (Luke 24:32).

Neither is prayer the end goal; it is rather the act of communicating with our loving God and Savior in an ever deepening and more vulnerable way. It's the avenue through which we say "I love You," the discipline by which we learn that he is always there to listen, the venue through which we bare our hearts. It's the place where we can shake our fist in frustration when we don't understand why he has allowed tragedy or hardship in our lives . . . and discover that he doesn't run away but beckons us with outstretched arms of love. It's the point at which we surrender and find the peace we have been searching for.

Attending church is our scrimmage game. When we meet together, we inspire, encourage, and comfort each other in our faith. The church is filled with real people who stumble, hurt, and are selfish. There we receive the opportunity to practice imitating Jesus, offering grace, and fighting Satan, just as our knight emulated his mentor.

If I've trained well, I'm ready to face my own every day, "real" world. I can anticipate the moves of my opponent, Satan, as I skillfully manipulate my weapons of praise, worship, and Bible truth. I have great endurance for the never-ending battles he brings to separate me from my Savior.

Let's train well to reach our goal, to love the Lord our God with all our heart, soul, mind, and strength.

Follow God's example, therefore, as dearly loved children and walk in the way of love.
EPHESIANS 5:1–2

Prayer: Lord, keep my eyes on the goal of my training—to encounter you. May I understand that the disciplines of prayer, Bible study, worship, and participation in church are tools, not the end goal.

Blessed is the one who trains well, for they shall enter the presence of the Lord with ease.

Day 36

Where, O death, is your sting?
1 CORINTHIANS 15:55

Jellyfish Sting

"THE JELLYFISH CAN still sting you even after it's dead, Grandma," my grandson informed me as we examined the remains of one of these mysterious ocean creatures. He cautioned me not to touch it or step on it. "But if we accidentally step on one, I learned how to take care of their sting." Once we finished inspecting, we made sure to steer clear of the rest of the unfortunate ones we saw stranded on the sand.

Each day since I arrived I had seen a handful of jellyfish washed ashore. The week after my grandson left, their numbers increased exponentially. I saw them about every five feet down the sand. I wondered why, and the carnage made me sad.

The translucent body gave me hints of the jellyfish's inside structure, but I could not see it clearly. It was blurred. That fact both fascinated and frustrated me. Finally, I walked past one whose loose balloon top sat askew, looking like a jaunty little hat tipped up sideways on his head. It allowed me to view the long tentacles tucked up beneath.

An experience at church this morning brought me back to pondering the blurry jellyfish. I put on my reading glasses to follow along as my pastor read a Bible passage. At the end I happened to glance up at him without removing the glasses. A cartoon-like image greeted me. His face was blurred to the point that it looked like a step-by-step drawing before the eyes, nose, and mouth had been added. I could make out a body outline with arms and legs and could see the colors of his clothes.

Despite the distortion, the translucence offered definitive clues to this person's identity. He acted like Pastor R with his distinctive hand gestures. The voice sounded identical. The colors on the fuzzy body seemed to be ones he often wore. He talked like, acted like, and dressed like my pastor. A glance over the top of the lenses verified that it was indeed him.

Death is blurry to me. I'm fascinated by what I do know of it and frustrated by what I don't. The Bible tells us a little bit, but not as much as I'd like. Here's what we do know from Revelation 21 and 22:

- We will be with Jesus after we die if we declare with our mouth, "Jesus is Lord" and "believe in [our] heart that God raised him from the dead" (Romans 10:9).
- Heaven sounds amazing. The Father and Jesus supply light 24/7. Night never comes, so there's no darkness, which means we'll have no need for a flashlight. We won't bump our shin during a midnight run to the bathroom (if we even need bathrooms). Alligators under the bed and boogeymen will no longer cause fear.
- We will see God's face though all eternity. No one on earth has ever seen God's face, except for Jesus. The name Emmanuel means "God with us," and Revelation 21:3 says, "Look! God's dwelling place is now among the people, and he will dwell *with* them. They will be his people, and God himself will be *with* them and be their God" (emphasis added). No more long-distance relationship.
- There will be no more death or mourning or crying or pain. God himself will wipe away any tears lingering on our cheeks from earth, where we have experienced all those results of a fallen world.

We know that death is a natural part of life, but that fact does not make it any easier for us to face the loss of a loved one. For some of us the sting of death is made worse by tragic circumstances surrounding a passing. My heart aches for those who have experienced this kind of tragedy.

Jesus experienced the pain of death as he wept for Lazarus (John 11) and observed the grief of Lazarus's sisters. His heart went out to the widow of Nain (Luke 7:11–16), and he spoke to the fear in Jairus and his wife (Mark 5:21–43).

Jesus's compassion reaches out to us, also, in our pain and fear. In addition to our not having our loved one accessible to us anymore, a part of us fears the unknown. We can't see what happened to them because we comprehend reality only as "a reflection as in a mirror" (1 Corinthians 13:12). This, dear friend, is the time to cling to the Bible's assurances, as we read above.

We believe that the words are from God because, just as I knew my pastor was really there when my glasses blurred his image, we know the sound of God's voice, recognize his actions, and witness the glory of his garments. He speaks truth. All of what we have just read about heaven sounds just like the Father whom Jesus modeled.

We may worry that our loved one didn't know Jesus as Savior. May I suggest, however, that we can never in this phase of eternity know what might have happened in their heart in the moments before death. We can choose to believe that they called upon Jesus.

The jellyfish can still sting us after it dies, but death can no longer sting us because of what Jesus did on the cross. Let's hold the hand of Jesus as he walks with us through the valley of the shadow of death (Psalm 23:4) pulling us close to his side. We can't at this time see everything we want to, but we can trust him.

Death has been swallowed up in victory.
1 CORINTHIANS 15:54

Prayer: Emmanuel, thank you for being with me. Affirm to me that what your Word says about heaven is true. Bring comfort to my grief-filled heart as I mourn those I have lost. Give me strength for each new day.

"Blessed are those who mourn, for they will be comforted." Matthew 5:4

Day 37

Let us consider how we may spur one another on toward love and good deeds.

HEBREWS 10:24

Cheering Each Other On

*T*HE MENTAL IMAGE of college kids on spring break can elicit disconcerting pictures of wild parties. Not so the small group of students who invaded Myrtle Beach during the third week of March. Singing around the sand fire pit into the wee hours of the morning constituted their most egregious "infraction." The respectful fun they enjoyed made it pleasant to have them around.

Late in the morning one day the college students entertained themselves, and observers, by racing each other down the beach. Jostling and laughter highlighted their fun as small groups lined up to run. Sand flew and cheers erupted. In one close race the winner stuck out his neck to win by a head. The boy's friends whooped and hollered enthusiastically, jumping up and down. As bystanders, we got caught up in their celebrations.

My daughters both ran track in high school. The younger one ran the 400 meter. Since it's a full-on sprint the whole way, she would hit the third turn and "hit a wall." At her request, her dad and I joined her coach at the third turn, where we screamed along with the crowd. She declared that only three voices reached her ears.

She heard her coach yelling, "Stride out!

She heard her dad yelling, "Watch your stride."

She heard me screaming, "You can do it. You can do it."

Our three voices gave her the motivation and grit to pour on the speed and keep going. Recently, she sent a video of my grandson running in an elementary school cross country meet. I could hear her voice at the finish line, screaming, "Go, go. You can do it. You're almost there." She shared later that he really speeds up when he hears cheering.

Now imagine the thunderous roar of cheers cascading out of a huge stadium with every inch of seating, along with standing room, filled. Energy vibrates with anticipation of victory. Voices chant, "Go, go, go! You've got this! You're almost there!" You suddenly realize that they are shouting for you as you run your life race. You were ready to give up, weary from the challenge, but now excitement rejuvenates your mind and body.

Where do I get such a silly idea? From Hebrews 12:1: "Since we are surrounded by such a great cloud of witnesses, let us throw off everything that hinders and the sin that so easily entangles. And let us run with perseverance the race marked out for us." The picture evoked is of an athletic stadium with the witnesses encouraging us.

Someone cheering us on can make the difference between our giving up or digging in with determination to win the race. Driving two thousand miles across the country to arrive in Myrtle Beach felt like a daunting "race." My stomach clenched and my neck tightened with each thought of the dreaded journey; yet, since I would be staying for a whole month, I wanted my car with me.

When my older daughter offered to drive out with me, I jumped at the chance. Do her go-to toddler words, "I can do it by myself," suggest why? She planned to drive out with me, stay for a couple of days, and then fly home. She cheered me on by standing with me in an area of fear and scaffolding the task to present manageable pieces for me. The drive became a pleasure because of her company and encouragement.

Once in Myrtle Beach, she cheered me on by making sure I was set up for success in my home away from home. We found grocery stores, gas stations, did an initial discovery drive around town, and explored the beach. By the time she left two days later, I felt completely safe.

Our life race is a marathon, not a sprint. Just as the friends of our college runner cheered for him so he would have the courage to stick out his neck, we can root for others in our lives.

"Hey, Sue, the love you show your patients (students, clients) is impacting their success."

"Judy, my son beamed all day from your comment that he had done a great job on his school project."

"Mary, thank you for listening and making me feel seen. It lifted the discouragement from me."

"Thanks, Bonnie. I couldn't have finished my project without your help."

For most of us, a simple recognition of our time and effort gives us the energy to keep on going. Life is often hard. To have someone acknowledge that we are navigating some part of it well can be a lifeline. We never know just how discouraged or depressed a person might be. Let's be free with our smiles, our hugs, and our affirming words. Let's help others to not grow weary and lose heart.

Let's also remember that Jesus roots for us along with the cloud of witnesses. "Let us run with perseverance the race marked out for us, fixing our eyes on Jesus, the pioneer and perfecter of faith" (Hebrews 12:1–2). In my mind, this verse depicts him standing there at the finish line where we can see him, yelling, "You can do it! Keep going! You're almost there!" Can you hear his voice?

*Encourage one another and build each other
up, just as in fact you are doing.*
1 THESSALONIANS 5:11

Prayer: Author of my faith, may I hear your voice as you motivate me to keep running my race, even when it feels difficult and endless. May you give me eyes to notice others around me who need encouragement.

*Blessed are those who encourage others around
them, for they shall be cheered on by God.*

Day 38

> *"The* Lord *bless you and keep you; the* Lord
> *make his face shine on you and be gracious to you;*
> *the* Lord *turn his face toward you and give you peace."*
>
> NUMBERS 6:24–26

The Ability to Bless

FEARLESSLY DARTING INTO the waves, the dogs leaped to catch large sticks flying through the air. With their "prey" clutched in their mouths, they swam back to shore. Heedless of the dripping water and sand, they deposited their treasure, instantly tense with anticipation for the next toss. Deep barks conveyed their joy. I laughed and laughed at their antics, especially when their owners had to dash out of the way as the dogs decided to shake off the water.

Smaller dogs on leashes trotted with squatty legs next to their owners in the shallow water. They sniffed passing dogs and people, their joyful yips carried away by the wind. As enamored with their play as were the larger dogs, they seemed almost to smile and laugh. Every day canine cavorting brought a smile to my face. Watching the love between owner and animal touched my spirit. The dogs brought joy and blessing to their humans.

An online sermon caught my attention one day after I had watched some playful dogs. I sat in my living room with a panoramic view of the water that merged with the horizon as the simple words penetrated my heart. Pastor Bo Stern of Beaverton Foursquare Church (March

2023) talked about how when we bless someone, we love without fear; we do good to someone and walk away without worry about how they have received the gift.

My old reaction would have been to panic with thoughts like, *How does a person do good and walk away without worrying about how the other person has received it? People-pleasing doesn't work that way. You must always over-analyze in advance how your words may affect someone else. Your "good" may appear offensive to them in some way, and they may even get mad at you and quit talking to you.*

The new me rejected those reactions. The dogs on the beach modeled what Bo had said. They lived in the moment and loved their owners with their yips and dog smiles. Concern over whether their love would be accepted or reciprocated didn't enter their minds. They expected their happy antics to be received with the same joy with which they were offered.

My good friend from Salem is like that. She invites people over for meals, takes on college students as adopted kids, and writes to soldiers. It never occurs to her that anyone would reject her overtures of love. And they never do. They soak up her listening ears, her nurturing heart, and her yummy cookies.

God tops even my friend. His outstretched hand reaches to all with the offer of love, adoption, and cleansing. He loves without fear. He is secure enough in himself that he knows that what he offers is truly good. Whether his gift is accepted or rejected is not a reflection on who he is.

Did you catch that? God is secure in himself. The difference between my fear or confidence in reaching out to others lies in how secure I feel in him. Whether someone accepts or rejects my gift is not a reflection of who I am.

My designer son-in-law has spent the last fourteen months personalizing the home that he and my daughter bought. Hand-created trim adorns the doors, windows, and massive fireplace wall. A hand-constructed outdoor kitchen has expanded the opportunities to use their gift of hospitality. He recently designed and built an outdoor "plant wall." Their goal is to have a home they can share with others.

With the same creative flair, care, and time my son-in-law has spent on his home, God designed my whole trip to Myrtle Beach. He had one main goal in mind: to make me secure enough in his love, and who he created me to be, that I would trust him explicitly. He wanted me to walk in partnership with him, approaching whatever he put before me with confidence, not fear.

We become secure in God when we internalize this verse: "We need have no fear of someone who loves us perfectly; his perfect love for us eliminates all dread of what he might do to us. If we are afraid, it is for fear of what he might do to us and shows that we are not fully convinced that he really loves us" (1 John 4:18 TLB).

What is holding you back from believing the truth that you don't need to fear him? What fear keeps you from reaching out to others? For most of us, it's the fear of rejection. Who wants to offer a part of themselves, only to have someone else ignore or decline our offering or even mock them?

Hear this truth. When God is the light of your life who guides your path, he guides you to those who need a blessing. When you give that smile or word of encouragement or offer to help with a need, you please him. Their acceptance or rejection of your blessings is usually about what is going on with them, not what they think of you.

One of my dearest friends appeared to reject my initial offers of friendship. I wanted to give up, but God directed me to persevere. Only later did I find out that she didn't believe anyone would want to be her friend. I'm so glad God prodded me to not back down. Don't give up, friend. The world needs you.

> *[The hearts of the righteous] are secure, they will have no fear.*
> PSALM 112:8

Prayer: God, may I rest secure in you, not in myself and my abilities. May I realize and accept that the skills and abilities I have are gifts from you; therefore, my security does not rest in the gift but in the Giver.

Blessed are those who put their trust in God, for their hearts will rest in safety and security.

Day 39

Every good and perfect gift is from above, coming down from the Father of the heavenly lights.

JAMES 1:17

Parting Gifts

MY NINTH-FLOOR CONDO balcony became my friend. It afforded an amazing view, allowing me to see the seascape for miles straight out. The shoreline remained visible for a mile or more in each direction down the beach, till it curved out of sight. I could even see the tip of a huge Ferris wheel miles away in the southern part of town.

From this perch I watched the tail end of several sunrises—and noticed a woman who watched from the sand every day. She would huddle in her beach chair with a red sweatshirt and cozy blanket, remaining there until early afternoon. Her cooler beside her kept her supplied with food as she read her book after the sun woke up.

During spring break, I heard the laughter of children as they played. Dogs barked and chased frisbees. Beachcomber friends trekked out on their daily treasure hunts. Seagulls soared through the air, while sandpipers hopped along the wet sand.

The balcony served as my shell storage and display stage. The deck chairs held me while I read books, ate meals, or watched passersby. High above the ground, the small area provided privacy and safety where I always felt secure, no matter which pastime I was pursuing.

A day or two before my time in the condo was to end, God sent a beautiful parting gift for me to watch, a finale of sorts. I was sitting, idly watching the beach, when I noticed people pointing out to sea. More and more people stopped, looked, and pointed.

I turned my eyes to see the cause of the excitement and to my amazement spotted a pod of dolphins frolicking in the water offshore. Despite my having paid for a dolphin cruise (Day 16) in a quest to see a whole pod, this spectacle was the way God chose to fulfill that desire. On the cruise we had seen only one lone porpoise so far away that he was hard to spot. Yet here, in the comfort of my own space, I had a bird's eye view of playful jumps and twists as four of the exquisite creatures interacted with each other.

Unbelievably, separated from the pod and as close to the shore as he could get without grounding, a lone dolphin gracefully arced in the sky before gliding effortlessly back into the water. No doubt existed in my mind that this fellow was "my" dolphin. The magnificence of these two separate displays equaled the pizzazz of a fireworks finale. They "shouted" in a braille audible only to me, "Farewell, beloved of God. May joy go with you as you return home." My heart was full.

In each gift God embedded a lesson for me. Today, as I began recounting my amazing parting gift, I wondered what hidden treasure awaited my belated discovery. So, I asked God.

When he brought my up-close and personal dolphin show, I sat in a front row seat where I could see the animal up close. Once my eyes were fixed in the right direction, the gift couldn't be missed. For the larger show, the animals "performed" at quite a distance. Details like facial features were not well defined, so I felt as if I were gazing at miniatures. This gift could easily have been missed if the crowds pointing fingers had not created an anticipation of discovering something unusual.

Sometimes God gives us obvious gifts that we can't miss. We stand in awe of them, and our grateful hearts shout thanksgiving. We share excitedly with our friends—and at times with anyone else who will listen—what God has done. In other instances, though, we glimpse God's gifts from a distance. We can easily miss them if we're not waiting with expectancy for the goodness of God to show up. From God's perspective the gifts are close, but from ours they can feel far removed.

Distance is relative. One of my grandsons received a little dog for Christmas last year. His tiny legs are only about six to eight inches long. My son-in-law, by contrast, has long legs and a large stride. When my son-in-law and the dog walk together, their perspective of distance is no doubt quite different. What feels like just a few steps to my son-in-law is a scramble for Bentley. The distance is the same, but the perspective and the effort to get there differ.

Messianic prophecies are scattered throughout the Old Testament. Generation after generation wondered whether Christ would come in their lifetime . . . and generation after generation died without seeing the promise fulfilled.

When Jesus finally arrived on earth, two expectant watchers recognized him immediately. God had told Simeon that he would not die until he had seen the Lord's Christ. On the day Mary and Joseph brought Jesus to be circumcised, Simeon was moved by the Holy Spirit to enter the temple courts. Upon seeing the child, Simeon instantly knew that his wait was over. He took Jesus in his arms, praising God and prophesying over his Son (Luke 2:25–25).

At that very moment the prophetess Anna came upon them, and she immediately perceived that she was seeing the Messiah. At eighty-four years old, Anna never left the temple but worshiped there night and day, fasting and praying (Luke 2:36–38). Her spirit had become so attuned to God that she recognized Jesus. May our spirits become so in tune with God that we see all his gifts—those close up and those viewed only from a distance.

> *In the morning, LORD, you hear my voice; in the morning*
> *I lay my requests before you and wait expectantly.*
> PSALM 5:3

Prayer: Father in heaven, open my eyes, my ears, and my heart to wait with anticipation for whatever gift or beauty you will reveal today. May I see your hand even in situations that seem difficult.

Blessed are those who see the conspicuous gifts God gives them, for they shall see gifts that are more obscure.

Day 40

Then, because so many people were coming and going that they did not even have a chance to eat, [Jesus] said to them, "Come with me by yourselves to a quiet place and get some rest."

MARK 6:31

Come Away with Me

AS I TOOK my last walk on the beach, immense gratitude welled up inside. Words could not begin to express how my time in Myrtle Beach had impacted my life. I savored all that I had come to love: seagulls, surf, sand, and shells. I tucked them in my heart for one last time and opened my arms with childlike joy and restored laughter.

Bittersweet feelings also arose. Early tomorrow morning I would drive away from this lifeline, this place of respite and rest. Life's daily activities would resume. Yet I knew I was not the same person who had arrived thirty days earlier. I was leaving not just refreshed but transformed—confident in God's ability to take care of me in every situation. Fear no longer resided in me, and I could see the future through the lens of faith and excitement.

You may know the Polynesian legend of Johnny Lingo and how many cows he paid as a dowry for his bride. (Different online versions of the legend vary slightly.) Johnny was a shrewd trader known for his bargaining skills. When it came time for him to choose a wife, he picked a woman he had loved since childhood. In the eyes of others, she was homely, or at least plain, and painfully shy.

The custom in the woman's village required the father and the groom to bargain for the dowry price. A beautiful woman might bring a price of three or four cows. A less sought after woman might garner only a single cow for her father. Johnny paid ten cows for his wife, which evoked laughter and mockery from the villagers. Didn't he know how plain this woman was?

Johnny took his bride to live on an island away from her village. When a visitor to his island saw Johnny's bride, he responded with astonishment. This beautiful, confident woman could not be the same one he had heard about.

When he questioned Johnny, Johnny replied with great wisdom: "Have you ever thought about what life is like for a one-cow wife? She lives with the knowledge that her husband considers her the least valuable woman in the village. Everyone knows. She hangs her head in shame. A four-cow wife knows how valuable her husband considers her to be and is treated accordingly by her husband and other villagers.

"A ten-cow wife realizes that her husband thinks of her as a queen. Never again will anyone question her value as a person. She begins to glow with that knowledge. She can walk and talk with the confidence that she is greatly loved."

I went to Myrtle Beach feeling myself to be a one-cow woman. I left as a ten-cow wife. It's amazing what thirty days in a "God spa" can do for you. I "ate" a steady diet of natural beauty and exercise. I received daily words of love and affirmation. My Father, Creator, and Friend lavished personalized gifts upon me that were designed to rebuild belief in my value to him. An occasional present of beauty, affirmation, or rebuilding blesses us greatly.

Thirty days of receiving those endless treasures transformed me into a "ten-cow wife." God showed me my value to him every single day for thirty days. That understanding didn't end when I got into the car the next morning. Now, eighteen months later, I awaken every morning still knowing I am precious in his sight. I now seek new adventures with excitement: traveling to see family and attend writers' conferences. God has brought new friends, both from conferences and from my new church.

Equally bittersweet is the fact that this book has come to an end. Writing these words has never been for me about the end product but about the journey of remembering. God has opened my heart and mind to an even greater depth with regard to what he has accomplished in the last eighteen months. Pondering life, the Bible, and love has filled me with excitement and new insights. That in itself has been an adventure. I look forward with anticipation to what he has in mind for me next.

I pray that, as you have read of God pouring out his love to me at the beach, he has poured his love out on you also, whoever and wherever you are. I pray that you have received rest and respite from this "beach in a book" and that someday you will find your own "Myrtle Beach," if you have not already done so. I am asking him to touch you, encourage you, and lead you forward in hope. I pray on your behalf for courage to surrender and for you to trust him for your next step. I pray for you to gain a hunger for him and an anticipation of what he has in mind for you. I pray for you to become a ten-cow wife in his presence, glowing with confidence and beauty. Dear Reader, may God go with you.

God did not send his Son into the world to condemn the world, but to save the world through him.
JOHN 3:17

Prayer: God of grace and mercy, fill me with courage to trust you enough to surrender my future to you, one step at a time. May you open my eyes to see the tangible, as well as intangible, gifts you have for me each day. I love you.

Blessed are those who follow Jesus when he says, "Come away with me," for they shall be transformed in his presence.

Heartfelt Thanks to . . .

Tim Beals from Credo House Publishing—for taking this manuscript and turning it into a book, for your patience with all of my questions, and for working to fit the finished product into the timeline I had hoped for.

Karen Neumair—for your expert mentoring at Mt. Hermon that shaped this book into a living, breathing whole, for your wisdom and encouragement, and for your patience with all my questions before and after Write to Publish and Mt. Hermon.

My prayer group—Lynn, Carol, Nancy, Patti, Krystyn, and Paula—for deepening my prayer life, walking with me through devastating times, praying for this book to come into existence, and some of you for critiquing pages for me.

Carol—for advice and critiquing, for constant prayer and encouragement to bring this book to completion, for offering friendship from the first moment we met.

Jackie—for nearly fifty years of friendship, for modeling the love of Jesus, for reading and critiquing this book and adding encouragement to keep me going. I love you, friend.

Robyn—for shredding my middle chapters that were awful and making them good, for fervent prayer for God to shine through as the Author behind the author of this book, and for reaching out to me at Write to Publish and offering a new, but deep friendship.

Cherie Wagner from Neue Thing—for encouragement after reading my first few devotionals back at the beginning and for networking me with a speaking opportunity and relationships with other writers.

Morgan—for all you have done for me over the last several years, for reading the first half of the manuscript, and for networking me with others.

Connie—for being a friend of the heart who causes me to think deeply about the things of God, for all your prayer and encouragement for life and for this book, and for critiquing many of the devotionals.

www.ingramcontent.com/pod-product-compliance
Lightning Source LLC
LaVergne TN
LVHW051524070426
835507LV00023B/3286